ERRATA to *Palestine in Transition*

NB: p. 72, lines 20-21:
    for 'to accomodate an illuminate the data provided by the Amarna archive. Syro-Palestinian . . .'
    read 'to accommodate and illuminate the data provided by the Amarna archive, Syro-Palestinian . . .'

p. 47, n. 8, l. 3: *for* 'despite the sharp' *read* 'despite their sharp'
p. 56, l. 2:   *for* 'below, pp. 72-81' *read* 'below, pp. 72-83'
p. 56, l. 42: *for* 'and *Politico*-legal' read 'and politico-legal'
p. 57, l. 24: *for* 'and *politico*-legal' *read* 'and politico-legal'
p. 59, l. 12: *for* 'bought to abolish' *read* 'fought to abolish'
p. 61, l. 30: *for* 'scientists' *read* 'social scientists'
p. 75, n. 33, l. 3: *for* '*apdu* Knudtzon' *read* '*apud* Knudtzon'

PALESTINE
IN TRANSITION:
THE EMERGENCE OF
ANCIENT ISRAEL

THE SOCIAL WORLD
OF BIBLICAL ANTIQUITY
SERIES

General Editor
James W. Flanagan

PALESTINE
IN TRANSITION

THE EMERGENCE OF
ANCIENT ISRAEL

Edited by
DAVID NOEL FREEDMAN *and* DAVID FRANK GRAF

Published in association with
The American Schools of Oriental Research
by
THE ALMOND PRESS
SHEFFIELD
1983

THE SOCIAL WORLD OF BIBLICAL ANTIQUITY SERIES, 2

PALESTINE IN TRANSITION:
THE EMERGENCE OF ANCIENT ISRAEL

THE ALMOND PRESS
in association with
THE AMERICAN SCHOOLS OF ORIENTAL RESEARCH

Copyright © 1983 The Almond Press

British Library Cataloguing in Publication Data:

Palestine in transition.—(The Social world of Biblical
antiquity; 2)
   1. Palestine—History—To 70 A.D.
   I. Freedman, David Noel   II. Graf, David Frank
   III. Series
   993'.01   DS121

   ISBN 0-907459-32-3
   ISBN 0-907459-33-1 Pbk

Published by
The Almond Press
P.O. Box 208
Sheffield S10 5DW
England

Printed in Great Britain by
Dotesios (Printers) Ltd
Bradford-on-Avon, Wiltshire

Contents

Introduction

The "rise and fall" of civilizations is a familiar theme in historiography, and a legitimate preoccupation. Even though normally any proposed interpretation of such problems is found to be vexatious and controversial, such transitions and changes clamor for explanation. This has especially been the case with ancient Israel's emergence in the late second millennium B.C., where the question of origins has been a traditional battleground of warring opinions, a result of the conflicting accounts in Joshua and Judges and the oblique archaeological evidence.

Since the appearance of George E. Mendenhall's seminal but rather laconic article on "The Hebrew Conquest of Palestine" (*Biblical Archaeologist* 25 [1962]: 66–87), an additional factor has been introduced to this already fierce debate, namely the application of modern social theory to the biblical accounts and material evidence. A ground swell of interest was soon generated in this radically different approach suggesting that "there was no real conquest of Palestine at all," but rather "a peasant's revolt against the network of interlocking Canaanite city states."

The present collection of essays represents a basically sympathetic attempt to reevaluate Mendenhall's original hypothesis from the perspective of developments during the last several decades. All of them were initially intended for the pages of the *Biblical Archaeologist* but because of their thematic similarity or length have been gathered together into the present volume. The historical background and setting for this reassessment of the Israelite tradition is provided by the essays of W. H. Stiebing, J. M. Halligan, and N. K. Gottwald, who probe and analyze, respectively, the political, social, and economic components of the "revolt" hypothesis. The latter two contributions represent revised versions of papers presented at the 112th annual meeting of the Society of Biblical Literature (see the *SBL Seminar Papers*, no. X, ed. G. MacRae [Missoula, MT: Scholars Press, 1976]: 145–169). This discussion forms the basis for M. L. Chaney's reevaluation of the traditional "conquest model" formulated by the Albright school and the "peaceful immigration" model developed by the German school of Albrecht Alt.[1] Chaney then examines the various criticisms of Mendenhall's thesis before developing his own view, an amended version of the "revolt" model supplemented by an emphasis on the frontier aspects of the rebellion.

After these essays were completed, Norman K. Gottwald's massive treatise *The Tribes of Yahweh: A Sociology of the Religion of Liberated*

---

[1]For recent statements of these views see the essays of M. Weippert, A. Malamat, and Y. Yadin in *Symposia celebrating the seventy-fifth anniversary of the founding of the American Schools of Oriental Research (1900–1975)*, ed. F. M. Cross (Cambridge, MA: American Schools of Oriental Research, 1979), pp. 15–68.

Israel, 1250–1050 B.C.E. (Maryknoll, NY: Orbis, 1979) was published; in it yet another distinctive adaptation was made of Mendenhall's original hypothesis. This volume is the focus of a review essay by Mendenhall himself, whose remarks make it clear that, in the past twenty years, his own views have undergone considerable refinement and modification. Even a cursory reading of this final entry to the volume will show that it is a mistake to criticize Mendenhall's interpretation of the events in the Late Bronze Age as simply a modern sociological theory superimposed on the biblical traditions. Neither will it be possible any longer to designate the "revolt model" as the "Mendenhall-Gottwald" hypothesis, as Mendenhall's comments about the incompatibility of their methodology will reveal.

In placing the developments of Palestine during the 13th and 12th centuries into a larger historical and geographical framework, Mendenhall again subjects the traditional views and some of the current theories to some severe criticism. As archaeological inquiry proceeds in the adjacent areas of Syria and Transjordan, it is becoming increasingly evident that what was formerly considered uniquely early Iron Age "Israelite" is only evidence of a larger culture that embraced the contemporary surrounding states. For example, such features as domestic architecture, ceramic forms, and agricultural practices, which have been produced from excavations at early Israelite sites, are now known to have been utilized or employed by the inhabitants of the adjacent regions.[2] Most of this evidence has only recently been made available and is only alluded to in Mendenhall's essay.

What can be concluded from these new developments is that the events that brought about the emergence of ancient Israel are far more complex than previously thought. Of course, the fragmentary nature of our sources and the failure of the archaeological and literary evidence to dovetail neatly into a consistent picture make it very difficult to prove that any of the proposed models or views is the correct one. The most that can be offered by any one interpretation is a more reasonable and satisfactory explanation of the evidence than the other theories can provide. If these essays then can

---

[2]The pottery formerly associated only with Israelite Iron Age settlements has been found at Sahab, east of Amman, in similar stratigraphical contexts. See M. Ibrahim, "The Collared-rim Jar of the Early Iron Age," *Archaeology in the Levant: Essays for Kathleen Kenyon*, ed. R. Moorey and P. Parr (Warminster, England: Aris & Phillips, 1978), pp. 116–26. The so-called "Israelite four-room house" also has been discovered on the Transjordanian plateau during the Moabite survey directed by J. Maxwell Miller of Emory University. For new finds of the so-called "Midianite pottery" discussed by Mendenhall, see M. L. Ingraham, et al., "Saudi Arabian Comprehensive Survey Program: Preliminary Report of the Northwestern Province (with a note on a brief survey of the Northern Province)," *ATLAL: The Journal of Saudi Arabian Archaeology* 5 (1981): 59–84, esp. 74–75. In this report, it is concluded that Midianite culture in the early Iron Age "extended from Qurayya as far as the Red Sea coastal wadis and the Gulf of Aqaba."

[3]M. I. Finley, *Aspects of Antiquity: Discoveries and Controversies* (New York, Viking, 1969), p. 6.

stimulate greater dialogue about this significant epoch of ancient Israel's history, the central aim of this volume will be accomplished. If this objective appears to be too limited, the words of M. I. Finley about the contemporary quest to understand the past may be recalled:

> The more precisely we listen and the more we become aware of its [the past's] pastness, even of its inaccessibility, the more meaningful the dialogue becomes. In the end, it can only be a dialogue in the present, about the present.[3]

April 1983   David Noel Freedman
Ann Arbor   David Frank Graf

The Amarna Period

WILLIAM H. STIEBING, JR.

The recent tours in France, England, and the United States of objects from Tutankhamun's tomb have reawakened public interest in the Amarna Period during which the boy-king lived. This era, the time of the pharaoh Akhenaton (ca. 1379–1362 B.C.) and his immediate successors, has been the most written-about period in Egyptian history. It was an age of revolution— in religion, in art, in Egyptian internal and foreign affairs. It has been celebrated as the age which produced the world's first truly monotheistic religion. Akhenaton has been called the first real individual in history. And some have sought the origins of Hebrew religion and nationhood in this time. No wonder, then, that the Amarna Period has held fascination for Egyptologists, art historians, and biblical scholars alike.

But the revolutionary changes of the Amarna era were regarded as heresies by later generations of Egyptians. The monuments from this time were smashed, the rulers' names destroyed, and all records and memories of the period suppressed. These actions helped cloak the age in an appealing aura of mystery, but they also destroyed the evidence needed for drawing firm conclusions about its history.

When in November of 1922 Howard Carter discovered the tomb of Tutankhamun, little was known about this 18th-Dynasty pharaoh except that he had reigned during the Amarna Period. However, unlike other Egyptian sepulchers, Tutankhamun's tomb was relatively intact. It had been entered twice in antiquity by tomb robbers, but in both instances the robberies seem to have been discovered quickly and the tomb had been resealed. The thieves made off with some jewelry and other small objects, but thousands of burial gifts remained. Surely, it was thought, such an abundance of material would provide much historical information on the life and times of this obscure ruler. Unfortunately, it did not. Carter's summary of the situation (1923 vol. 1: 44–45) remains true today:

> What do we really know about this Tut.Ankh.Amen with whom we have become so surprisingly familiar? Remarkably little, when you come right down to it. In the present state of our knowledge we might say that the one outstanding feature of his life was the fact that he died and was buried.

Sad to say, we know little more about Tutankhamun's immediate predecessors. We cannot even be sure of his relationship to Akhenaton, the driving force behind the Amarna revolution.

TUTANKHAMUN'S PARENTAGE AND THE COREGENCY PROBLEM

Examination of Tutankhamun's mummy showed that he was about 18 or 19 years old when he died after a nine year reign. Thus, he must have been only a 9 or 10 year old child when he became pharaoh. What was his claim to the throne? Who was his father and who was his mother? No one knows for sure. A recently discovered inscription describes him as "son of the king, of his body." So, Tutankhamun was a member of the royal family by birth and not just by marriage. However, the name of the king who was his father is not given, and the identity of Tutankhamun's father has important implications for the way one reconstructs events of the Amarna Age.

Among the objects in Tutankhamun's tomb were two miniature coffins, one containing a small gold statuette thought by some to represent Amenhotep III and the other a lock of hair from Tiy, Amenhotep III's Great Wife (or Queen). Possibly these were mementos of the boy-king's parents. Even more important are inscriptions at the entrance of Tutankhamun's colonnade at Luxor and on two lions from a temple of Amun at Soleb in Nubia. On these monuments Tutankhamun refers to Amenhotep III as his father.

One might think that this evidence would settle the issue, but it is not quite that simple. The miniature coffins from the tomb do not have inscriptions relating their contents to Tutankhamun's father and mother; they could as easily be mementos of his grandparents as of his parents. In the tomb there were also objects bearing the names of other predecessors of the young king, even that of Thutmose III whose reign had occurred a century before Tutankhamun's. To single out the mementos of Amenhotep III and Tiy as evidence of Tut's parentage is rather arbitrary. In fact, the small statuette ascribed to Amenhotep III is more likely an image of Tutankhamun himself.

The Luxor and Soleb inscriptions are better evidence, but they do not clinch the case. The word translated "father" in these texts also could be used to mean "ancestor" during this period of Egyptian history. These inscriptions show that Tutankhamun claimed descent from Amenhotep III, but by themselves they cannot prove that Amenhotep III was Tut's father rather than his grandfather.

X-ray studies of the mummies of Tutankhamun and Amenhotep III have revealed few similarities between them, suggesting the conclusion that Amenhotep III could *not* be Tutankhamun's father. Unfortunately, this scientific evidence also is not conclusive. The mummy which bears Amenhotep III's name was found in a cache of royal mummies which had been gathered together, rewrapped, and labeled by 21st Dynasty priests after many of the royal tombs had been robbed. In the confusion of handling many damaged corpses from different tombs, the priests may have mis-

labeled some of the bodies. The mummy which bears the name of Amenhotep III is one of those which is suspect.

Textual evidence shows that Amenhotep III had a long reign of 38 or
39 years, and there is no indication that he was a minor when he acceded to
the throne. But the mummy bearing his name was only between 40 and 50
years old at death. It not only shows no physical similarity to Tut's
mummy, but it also displays no resemblance to the body of Thutmose IV,
Amenhotep III's father. Furthermore, the embalming technique used on
this mummy is unique for the 18th and 19th Dynasties. Resin and linen had
been packed in the mouth and under the skin of the neck, arms, and legs to
give a more lifelike appearance to the dessicated body. Such embalming
became common in the 21st and 22nd Dynasties, but the mummy of
Amenhotep III is the only one earlier than the late 20th Dynasty to exhibit
this interesting technique. The lack of family resemblance between the
mummies of Amenhotep III and Tutankhamun is just further evidence that
the body thought to be that of Amenhotep III was mislabeled by the
priests. It probably belongs to a late 20th or early 21st Dynasty ruler. So,
the scientific "proof" that Amenhotep III was *not* Tut's father is no more
valid than the inscriptional "proof" that he was.

If Tutankhamun was the son of Amenhotep III and Tiy there must
have been a considerable overlap between the 38-year reign of Amenhotep III and the 17-year rule of Akhenaton. The existence of such an
overlap or coregency naturally would affect the interpretation of the
evidence of the Amarna revolution. While a number of scholars have
argued in favor of such a coregency, they have not been able to agree on its
length. Most of the evidence they cite consists of reliefs showing Amenhotep III and Akhenaton together, both wearing the insignia of kingship.
There are also objects from Amarna (the present name for Akhenaton's
capital, Akhetaton) bearing the names of Amenhotep III and Tiy, suggesting that they lived there for a time. Such evidence, though, is not very
convincing. It is known that there was a cult to the deified Amenhotep III,
and the reliefs in question can be interpreted as Akhenaton making
offerings or prayers to his deceased father. Offering tables and other
objects from Amarna bearing the name of Amenhotep III also can be
explained in terms of the cult to the dead king. The possibility of such
alternative explanations for the material cited to demonstrate a period of
joint rule between Akhenaton and Amenhotep III, when combined with the
evidence making an overlap in their reigns unlikely, has caused most
Egyptologists to reject the coregency hypothesis.

Letters to Akhenaton from the Hittite king and the ruler of Mitanni
expressing their condolences over Amenhotep III's death suggest that
Akhenaton became pharaoh only after his father died. The foreign rulers
assumed that the new pharaoh knew little or nothing about the past
diplomatic exchanges between Amenhotep III and their respective king-

doms. In fact, Tushratta, king of Mitanni, suggested that Akhenaton ask his mother, Queen Tiy, about the former relationship between Mitanni and Egypt. It is very unlikely that Tushratta would have written such a thing to a man who had been coruler with his father for a number of years, even if he knew that Akhenaton had been the junior partner in the government and had left all diplomacy to his father. Also, Tushratta's three letters to Akhenaton indicate that fairly long intervals of time occurred between them. It is difficult to fit these letters, as well as the many others from vassal princes of Palestine-Syria, into the relatively short period of sole rule Akhenaton would have had if his reign had overlapped considerably with that of his father.

More significant, though, is the complete absence of double datings—monuments or events dated to year x of Amenhotep III and year y of Akhenaton. If there was a coregency, we must assume that two conflicting sets of dates were used, some things being dated according to Amenhotep III's regnal years and others from Akhenaton's accession. It is difficult to believe that the Egyptian bureaucracy could have functioned under such a confusing system, especially when one notes that many objects (dockets on wine jars, for instance) contain a regnal year but not the name of the king in question.

The coregency hypothesis runs into a similar problem in dealing with the names of Egyptian high officials of the time. Many of the men who held office under Amenhotep III are different from those who occupied the same positions under Akhenaton. If the two kings ruled jointly there must have been two bureaucracies, one centered at Thebes (or Memphis) and the other at Akhenaton's city, Akhetaton. How such a dual system could work is a mystery.

A coregency between Amenhotep III and Akhenaton, then, is extremely unlikely. Akhenaton probably came to the throne upon his father's death and reigned independently for 17 years. This means that Akhenaton must be the unnamed king who was Tutankhamun's father.

Often it has been asserted that Akhenaton had no sons, only six daughters. However, such statements are almost certainly incorrect. Akhenaton and his Great Wife, Nefertiti, had only daughters, but Akhenaton had other wives who are rarely mentioned in texts or portrayed on monuments. It was customary for pharaohs to have harems, and we know that Akhenaton inherited at least one wife from the harem of his father. The woman in question was Taduhepa, daughter of the king of Mitanni. She had been sent as a bride to Amenhotep III during his last years, and when Amenhotep III died Tushratta gave her to Akhenaton. How many children Akhenaton had by his minor wives is unknown. It is likely, though, that he did have children by one or more of them, and that at least *two* of these children were boys. Letters to Akhenaton from the kings of Babylon, Mitanni, the Hittites, and Alashiya (probably Cyprus) refer to "your sons" a number of times. These kings must have had some knowledge of the

Egyptian court; it is unlikely that they would have asked about the welfare of nonexistent princes. So the myth that Akhenaton fathered only daughters should be quietly buried and forgotten.

When Tutankhamun's mummy was first studied, pathologists noted its close resemblance to a male body discovered in a small tomb in the Valley of the Kings in 1907. This badly preserved corpse had been found lying in a coffin originally made for one of Akhenaton's daughters but modified to serve for a king. The king's name had been obliterated wherever it occurred on the coffin and on the mummy's gold wrapping bands. These facts, together with the presence in the tomb of some objects bearing traces of Akhenaton's name (also erased), led some Egyptologists to conclude that the body was that of Akhenaton. However, medical studies showed that this king had been only 20–25 years old at death—too young for Akhenaton. But this age was about right for Smenkhkare, a little-known pharaoh who occupied the throne very briefly between the reigns of Akhenaton and Tutankhamun. Smenkhkare's parentage, like that of Tutankhamun, is unknown. but recent X-ray studies and blood tests have confirmed the close genetic relationship between the mummies of these two young kings. Smenkhkare and Tutankhamun were probably full brothers, both sons of Akhenaton and one of his minor wives.

We can only guess at the identity of Tutankhamun's mother. The monuments of Akhenaton's reign emphasize the king's Great Wife, Nefertiti, and her daughters almost exclusively. This fact makes more significant the discovery of inscriptions dedicated to Kia, the "great beloved wife" of Akhenaton. Was Kia singled out from the rest of the harem for such special honor because she was the mother of the crown prince, Smenkhkare, and his younger brother, Tutankhamun? Possibly, but we can only speculate. There is no solid evidence supporting such a conclusion.

All we know for certain is that Tutankhamun was the son of a king. It is probable that Smenkhkare was his brother and that Akhenaton was his father. Perhaps his mother was Kia, a member of Akhenaton's harem. But the controversial and speculative nature of these statements demonstrates just how little Tutankhamun's intact burial site has done to clear up the mysteries surrounding the Amarna Period.

THE REIGN OF AKHENATON

When Amenhotep III died, his son Amenhotep IV, became pharaoh of Egypt. From the beginning of his reign the new king emphasized the worship of the Aton (the name for the sun disc), and erected a temple to him near Amun's temple at Thebes. The ancient sun god Re had been worshipped on occasion under the name of the Aton by Amenhotep III and some of his 18th Dynasty predecessors, so the dedication of a temple to Aton was not a revolutionary act. However, Amenhotep IV did break with tradition by having grotesque statues of himself (which probably were exaggerated caricatures of his true appearance) placed within the temple.

Previous pharaohs had been depicted as perfectly proportioned, godlike rulers. These statues of Amenhotep IV showed an ugly, thin-faced king with fleshy lips, an oversized jaw, skinny neck, narrow and sloping shoulders, effeminate breasts, protruding abdomen, fleshy hips and thighs, and spindly lower legs. In this temple Amenhotep IV also went beyond the bounds of tradition in his emphasis on his Great Wife, Nefertiti. She was depicted as a goddess, the equal of her divine husband.

Some scholars look at the portraits of the deformed king and see the face of a genius—a religious mystic whose physical limitations turned his attention inward to the spiritual realm. They see a prophet who would proclaim belief in a universal, loving deity. Others look at the same portraits and conclude that Amenhotep IV was mentally retarded. With such physical deformities (including his misshapen skull), they claim, he could not have had normal intelligence and could not have been responsible for the revolutionary changes of the Amarna period. His wife or his mother must have been masterminding the entire revolution from behind the scenes.

Later statues do not emphasize the king's physical deformities as much as the earliest ones do, and it is probable that whatever physical impairments he had, they did not affect his mind. If Amenhotep IV had been only a figurehead with Tiy or Nefertiti making the decisions, it is safe to say there would have been no revolution. Surely the person behind the scenes would take care to present an appearance of normality in the royal family. It would be important that no one suspect that the king was a mental defective. Neither Tiy nor Nefertiti would have emphasized the king's true state by erecting the grotesque portraits of Amenhotep IV in the Aton temple. And they would not have broken with tradition by emphasizing the role of Nefertiti. Only Amenhotep himself could and would have given the order to his artists to violate the traditional way the king was portrayed. While his mother and his wife may have supported his efforts, Amenhotep IV must be granted primary responsibility for the Amarna revolution.

For the first few years of his reign, though, the strange portraits and increased emphasis on his wife seem to have been the only serious breaks with the past. Then, in his fourth regnal year, about halfway between Memphis and Thebes, Amenhotep IV began building for his god a new city— Akhetaton, "the Horizon of the Aton." Two years later he changed his name from Amenhotep ("Amun is satisfied") to Akhenaton (probably "the Effective Spirit of the Aton"), and he moved his family and the court to the new capital.

As time passed Akhenaton's conception of the Aton became more abstract and his worship of the sun god more exclusive. About his eighth or ninth year the official name of the Aton was altered to remove from it the hieroglyphs symbolizing the sun as a falcon. At the same time words like "truth" and "mother" began to be spelled out phonetically instead of being expressed ideographically by hieroglyphs which could also be read as divine names. Later, probably sometime between years 9 and 12, Akhenaton closed the temples of all of the traditional gods of Egypt. The names of the proscribed deities were hacked off monuments, and the sacred images were destroyed. Especially hated was the name of Amun, which was erased wherever it was found, even in the name of Akhenaton's father, Amenhotep III.

At Akhetaton the royal family worshipped the Aton as the sole god, the creator of all things. The great hymn to the Aton (Wilson, 1955a: 370), found in the tomb of Ay, praises the sun god in phrases which often have been compared to Psalm 104:

Thou appearest beautifully on the horizon of heaven,
Thou living Aton, the beginning of life!
When thou art risen on the eastern horizon,
Thou hast filled every land with thy beauty. . . .

When thou settest in the western horizon,
The land is in darkness, in the manner of death. . . .
Darkness *is a shroud*, and the earth is in stillness,
For he who made them rests in his horizon. . . .

How manifold it is, what thou hast made!
They are hidden from the face (of man).
O sole god, like whom there is no other!
Thou didst create the world according to thy desire,
Whilst thou wert alone:
All men, cattle, and wild beasts,
Whatever is on earth, going upon (its) feet,
And what is on high, flying with its wings.
The countries of Syria and Nubia, the *land* of Egypt,
Thou settest every man in his place,
Thou suppliest their necessities:
Everyone has his food, and his time of life is reckoned.

Many have seen this new religion as a monotheistic faith on the order of later Judaism, Christianity, and Islam. And some biblical scholars have claimed that Akhenaton's faith influenced the development of Israelite monotheism. But there are varying theories about how the two faiths are related. The biblical statement (Exod 1:11) that the Israelites had to build the cities of Pithom and Raamses (which were constructed in the 13th century B.C.) makes it difficult to place Moses in the Amarna period and make him a disciple of Akhenaton. However, the widely accepted 13th century date for the Exodus is only a century after Akhenaton's death. It has been surmised that during that century Akhenaton's beliefs were preserved at Heliopolis, the ancient Egyptian center of sun worship, and that it was there that the concept of monotheism was transmitted to Moses.

But those who hold such ideas usually neglect an important aspect of the Amarna religion—the position of Akhenaton. The Aton hymn makes it

clear that the king was the intermediary between man and the Aton
(Wilson, 1955a: 371):

> There is no other that knows thee
> Save thy son Neferkheperure Waenre [Akhenaton],
> For thou hast made him well-versed in thy plans and in thy strength. . . .
> [*Everything is*] made to flourish for the king. . . .
> Since thou didst found the earth
> And raise them up for thy son,
> Who came forth from thy body:
> The King of Upper and Lower Egypt. . . .
> Akhenaton, . . . and the Chief Wife of the King . . .
> Nefertiti, living and youthful forever and ever.

The well-ordered world which Aton created provided for the general
needs of all mankind, but special favors or individual blessings came only
through the divine couple on earth. Inscriptions show that courtiers and
citizens of Akhenaton addressed prayers to the Aton's earthly embodiment,
Akhenaton, and to his divine wife, Nefertiti. When individuals prayed
directly to the Aton, it was usually to ask for continued blessings on the
royal family whose welfare was deemed so necessary for the prosperity and
well-being of Egypt.

Thus, the common description of Akhenaton's religion as monotheism
is incorrect. There were three gods in the Amarna faith—Aton, Akhenaton,
and Nefertiti. and it was only through the divine couple on earth that
ordinary people approached the Aton. Only those with direct and constant
access to the king and queen could have drawn much solace from such a
religion; it is not surprising that it failed to take root in the hearts of most
Egyptians.

The many differences in detail, as well as in basic concepts, between
Akhenaton's religion and the Yahwism of early Israel make a direct
relationship between the two unlikely. There is a definite similarity between
the Aton hymn and Psalm 104, but phrases used in that hymn were applied
to other Egyptian gods after Akhenaton's death. It was probably these later
hymns, perhaps mediated by Canaanite sources, which influenced the
psalmist long after the end of the Amarna age.

Another frequently cited connection between the Amarna period and
the Bible is the presence in Syria and Palestine during this time of a group
of people called *ḫabiru* or *ḫapiru*. They are mentioned in the Amarna
letters as enemies of Egypt who took over portions of the pharaoh's
empire. H. H. Rowley and Theophile J. Meek, among others, have
identified these attacks by the *ḫabiru* with at least one phase of the Hebrew
conquest of Palestine.

However, study of all the texts mentioning the *ḫabiru* (which probably
should be read as *ʿapiru*) has shown that this term signified a *class* of
people with diverse ethnic origins. It was not a gentilic term as "Hebrew" is
in the Bible. The *ʿapiru* were uprooted, stateless individuals who became

seasonal agricultural workers, mercenaries, slaves, or bandits, depending upon circumstances. There is no indication in the Amarna letters that the *apiru* had a tribal organization or that different groups of them were cooperating with one another. While some of Israel's ancestors may have come from the ⁽apiru class, it is unlikely that the activities of the marauding groups of the Amarna period can be equated with any portion of the Israelite conquest of the Holy Land.

Our knowledge of the last five years of Akhenaton's reign is even more confused and uncertain than it is for the rest of the Amarna period. A little after year 12 Meketaton, the second daughter of Akhenaton and Nefertiti, died. Reliefs showing the royal couple mourning over their daughter's body are the last to depict Nefertiti. Some scholars have surmised that she and Akhenaton quarreled over the king's religious policy, that Nefertiti was removed from her position as queen, and banished to the northern part of the city. There is really no valid evidence for this view, however. It is likely that the queen died within a year or two after the burial of Meketaton. Queen Tiy must have passed away about this time also.

Akhenaton then seems to have married his oldest daughter, Meritaton, elevating her to her mother's former position. On a few monuments which were in their final stages of completion when these events occurred, Nefertiti's name was replaced by that of Meritaton. But there was no widespread excision of Nefertiti's name and image from older monuments as there probably would have been if she had fallen from the king's favor.

Perhaps the deaths of his daughter, Great Wife, and mother caused Akhenaton to consider his own mortality and to take steps to provide for the succession. He named his son, Smenkhkare, coregent. Since he was not the son of Akhenaton's Great Wife, Smenkhkare's claim to the throne was probably strengthened by having him marry Meritaton. Smenkhkare took Nefertiti's place as the third deity in the Amarna religion. He adopted the name Neferneferuaton ("Beautiful is the Beauty of the Aton") which had been used for Nefertiti from the sixth year of Akhenaton onward, and he incorporated into his name the epithet "beloved of Waenre [Akhenaton]."

For his part, after giving his current Great Wife to his son and coregent, Akhenaton married his next oldest daughter, Ankhesenpaaton. Akhenaton's new queen was only about 13 years old. Nevertheless, sometime during the two, or two and a half, years of her marriage to her father, Ankhesenpaaton bore him a daughter.

It is possible that Akhenaton now recognized the failure of his religious revolution and sent Smenkhkare to Thebes to make peace with the remnants of the priesthood of Amun. A graffito in a Theban tomb makes it certain that by the third year of Smenkhkare the worship of Amun had been reinstituted at Thebes. But this graffito is dated by the reign of Smenkhkare alone, making it likely that Akhenaton was dead at the time it was written. So we cannot be sure that Akhenaton ever compromised his religious beliefs or recognized the futility of his attack on

Egypt's 2,000-year-old traditions. The reconciliation with Amun may have taken place only after Akhenaton's death.

The heretic pharaoh died in his 17th year on the throne, and within about 6 or 8 months his young coregent followed him to the grave. Meritaton also seems to have died within the last year or so of her father's reign. The rapid succession of these royal deaths and the youth of Smenkhkare and Meritaton has led some to suspect foul play. However, since the succession remained within the Amarna family, it is more likely that the deaths were due to natural causes.

THE RESTORATION OF AMUN

The throne now passed to Tutankhaton ("the Living Image of the Aton" or "Perfect is the Life of the Aton"). The 9 year old king's claim to the throne was bolstered by having him marry his 15 or 16 year old half-sister, Ankhesenpaaton. Of course, Tutankhaton was too young to actually rule the country. The government was in the hands of Ay, probably the father of Nefertiti, Master of the Horse under Akhenaton, and now vizier and regent for the child pharaoh.

One of the first duties of the new pharaoh was to provide for the burial of his predecessor. Smenkhkare had been on the throne for such a short time that he probably had not been able to amass a large collection of funerary objects. Some of what he had collected, though, was not used for his burial. For example, miniature gold coffins made to hold Smenkhkare's internal organs were found in Tutankhamun's tomb. The original royal names had been erased and Tutankhamun's name substituted. A shrine made for Queen Tiy and a coffin and canopic jars made for one of the Amarna princesses were taken from storage and modified to serve for Smenkhkare's burial. Ay must have decided that his obligation to prepare a collection of burial goods for the living pharaoh's future use was more important than his duty to the deceased king.

Smenkhkare's policy of reconciliation with the old faith continued, but for the first three years of the new reign the court remained at Akhetaton. It was not enough, however, for the royal family merely to acquiesce to the people's worship of the old gods. A more positive step was needed to bridge the chasm which Akhenaton's rule had created between the king and his subjects. So the young pharaoh and his queen changed their names to Tutankh*amun* and Ankhesen*amun* respectively. They moved to the old royal palace at Memphis and abandoned Akhetaton. Without the pharaoh and royal court to sustain it, Akhenaton's city quickly became a ghost town.

Under Ay's direction Tutankhamun instituted a widespread building program to repair the temples damaged by Akhenaton (Wilson 1955b: 251–52):

Now when his majesty appeared as king, the temples of the gods and goddesses from Elephantine [down] to the marshes of the Delta [had . . .] gone to pieces. Their shrines had become desolate, had become *mounds* overgrown with [*weeds*]. Their sanctuaries were as if they had never been. Their halls were a footpath. The land was topsy-turvy, and the gods turned their backs upon this land. . . .

    This his majesty made monuments for the gods, [fashioning] their cult-statues of genuine fine gold from the highlands, building their sanctuaries anew as monuments for the ages of eternity, established with possessions forever, setting for them divine offerings as a regular daily observance, and provisioning their food-offerings upon earth.

New priests and prophets were appointed from the nobility. Singers, dancers, and slaves belonging to the palace were given to the temples. Revenues which had been diverted into the royal treasury or to temples of Aton during Akhenaton's reign were returned to the temples of local gods. New barques were constructed to carry the cult-statues across the Nile during festivals. Everything was restored to the way it has been before the Amarna revolution.

While the old religion was reinstituted and Amun resumed his position of primacy in the pantheon, the Aton continued to be worshipped. The Aton temples erected by Akhenaton remained open, and objects displaying the image or name of the Aton continued to be used. A gold-plated throne found in Tutankhamun's tomb depicts in Amarna style the king and queen under the protective rays of the Aton. Both the king's Amun and Aton names were used on different parts of the throne. No attempt was made to alter or destroy this evidence of continued Aton worship. But now the Aton was once again only one god among many, and he was no longer the pharaoh's favorite.

The Egyptian empire also had to be restored. The Amarna letters from Akhenaton's reign give evidence of revolts and internecine fighting among Egypt's vassals in Palestine and Syria. So, early in Tutankhamun's reign his general, Horemhab, seems to have undertaken a campaign to reestablish order in the area.

On a painted wooden box Tutankhamun is shown triumphing over Nubians and Asiatics, suggesting that after he reached adulthood at age 16 he may have personally led military expeditions into Nubia to the south, as well as into Palestine-Syria. These paintings have usually been regarded as copies of traditional scenes of the pharaoh defeating his enemies rather than as depictions of actual events in Tutankhamun's reign. But recent study of the young king's mummy has necessitated a reevaluation of this evidence. X-rays have revealed that Tutankhamun died from a wound near his left ear which fractured his skull and caused a cerebral hemorrhage. While such an injury could have been accidental, it was more probably the result of battle. Tutankhamun was 18 or 19 when he died, certainly old enough to assume personal leadership of Egypt's armies. There is no compelling reason, then, to doubt the essential historicity of the paintings showing Tutankhamun leading his forces in battle. The boy pharaoh who had reestablished Egypt's traditional religion probably gave his life trying to restore her traditional empire as well.

THE END OF THE AMARNA FAMILY

Tutankhamun died childless. In his tomb there were two mummified fetuses which may have been his and Ankhesenamun's stillborn children. But it is also possible that these bodies were placed in the tomb in connection with magical rites to ensure that the king would be reborn in the next world. Whatever the explanation for these small mummies, it is clear that Tutankhamun left no successors. He was the last male member of the long line of warrior pharaohs who had ruled Egypt since the expulsion of the Hyksos some two centuries earlier.

The lack of a male heir meant that whoever married Ankhesenamun would become pharaoh. There must have been some pressure for the queen to marry one of her vigorous and competent high officials such as the general Horemhab. Ankhesenamun, though, had other ideas. She wrote to the Hittite king, Shuppiluliumash, who like the Egyptian rulers claimed descent from the sun god (Goetze 1955):

> My husband died and I have no son. People say you have many sons. If you were to send me one of your sons, he might become my husband. I am loath to take a servant of mine and make him my husband.

Shuppiluliumash could not believe such an offer was genuine. So he sent a messenger to Egypt to secure reliable information. When he discovered that Ankhesenamun was in earnest, he complied with her request. It was too late, however. Someone (probably Horemhab) had learned of the plan. The young Hittite prince was murdered during his journey to Egypt.

In despair Ankhesenamun married Ay (who was probably her grandfather). Ay officiated at the burial rites as the body of Tutankhamun was laid to rest in a small tomb in the Valley of the Kings. Then he continued the implementation of those policies of restoration and reconciliation which he had initiated as Tutankhamun's regent. But Ankhesenamun's attempt to keep the royal power in the hands of the Amarna family was doomed to failure. Ay was already an old man when he became pharaoh, and he had no sons. He died after a brief reign of four or five years, leaving Egypt's throne up for grabs once again.

Horemhab became pharaoh, legitimizing his rule by marrying Ay's daughter, Mutnedjmet. Perhaps to win popular support and to strengthen his somewhat tenuous hold on the throne, the new pharaoh began a campaign of vengeance against the Aton. The Aton temples were destroyed, Akhetaton was razed to the ground, and inscriptions mentioning the Aton or Akhenaton were obliterated. Agents even entered the tombs of Akhenaton and Smenkhkare, hacking out images and names of the Aton and the two heretical kings. All mention of the Amarna pharaohs was avoided in official texts.

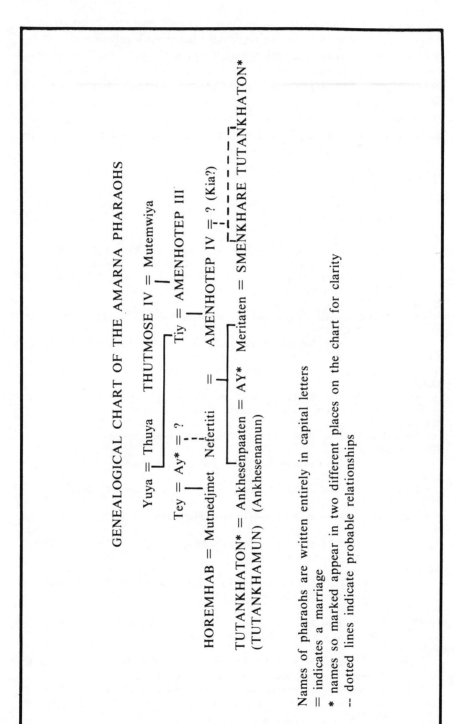

GENEALOGICAL CHART OF THE AMARNA PHARAOHS

Yuya = Thuya   THUTMOSE IV = Mutemwiya

Tiy = AMENHOTEP III

Tey = Ay* = ?   AMENHOTEP IV = ? (Kia?)

HOREMHAB = Mutnedjmet   Nefertiti =

TUTANKHATON* = Ankhesenpaaten = AY*   Meritaten = SMENKHARE TUTANKHATON*
(TUTANKHAMUN)   (Ankhesenamun)

Names of pharaohs are written entirely in capital letters
= indicates a marriage
* names so marked appear in two different places on the chart for clarity
-- dotted lines indicate probable relationships

Horemhab usurped monuments and statues built by Tutankhamun and Ay—their names were removed and Horemhab's substituted. But he did not violate Tutankhamun's burial. Perhaps the boy king's connection with the restoration of Amun saved his tomb from suffering the fate that befell those of Akhenaton and Smenkhkare. Despite two later attempts to rob it, Tutankhamun's tomb guarded its treasures down to modern times. It remains a unique testimony to the wealth and glory of pharaonic Egypt, and a witness (though one not as articulate as we might like) to the failure of a religious revolution and the end of an era.

BIBLIOGRAPHY

Alfred, C.
  1968   *Akhenaten, Pharaoh of Egypt: A New Study.* New York: McGraw-Hill.
  1975   Egypt: The Amarna Period and the End of the Eighteenth Dynasty. Pp. 49–97 in *The Cambridge Ancient History*, ed. I. E. S. Edwards, *et al.* 3rd ed. Vol. II/2. Cambridge: Cambridge University.
Campbell, E. F.
  1964   *The Chronology of the Amarna Letters.* Baltimore: Johns Hopkins.
Carter, H., and Mace, A. C.
  1923–33 *The Tomb of Tut.Ankh.Amen.* 3 vols. London, New York: Cassell.
Giles, F. J.
  1970   *Ikhnaton: Legend and History.* London: Hutchinson.
Goetze, A.
  1955   Suppululiumas and the Egyptian Queen. P. 319 in *Ancient Near Eastern Texts*, ed. J. B. Pritchard. 2nd ed. Princeton: Princeton University.
Greenberg, M.
  1955   *The Ḫab/piru.* New Haven, CT: American Oriental Society.
Harris, J., and Weeks, K.
  1973   *X-raying the Pharaohs.* New York: Charles Scribner's Sons.
Knudtzon, J. A.
  1908–15 *Die El-Amarna Tafeln.* 2 vols. Leipzig: Vorderasiatische Bibliothek.
Mercer, S. A. B., ed.
  1939   *The Tell el-Amarna Tablets.* Toronto: MacMillan.
Redford, D. B.
  1967   *History and Chronology of the Eighteenth Dynasty of Egypt: Seven Studies.* Toronto: University of Toronto.
Samson, J. A.
  1972   *Amarna, City of Akhenaton and Nefertiti: Key Pieces from the Petrie Collection.* London: Aris and Phillips.
Wente, E. F.
  1976   *Tutankhamun and His World.* Pp. 19–31 in *Treasures of Tutankhamun*, ed. I. E. S. Edwards, *et al.* New York: Ballantine.
Wilson, J. A.
  1955a   The Hymn to the Aton. Pp. 369–71 in *Ancient Near Eastern Texts*, ed. J. B. Pritchard. 2nd ed. Princeton: Princeton University.
  1955b   Tut-ankh-Amon's Restoration after the Amarna Revolution. Pp. 251–52 in *Ancient Near Eastern Texts*, ed. J. B. Pritchard. 2nd ed. Princeton: Princeton University.
  1973   Akh-en-Aton and Nefert-iti. *Journal of Near Eastern Studies* 32: 235–41.

The Role of the Peasant in the Amarna Period

JOHN M. HALLIGAN

Any description of Canaanite society in the literature of the second millennium B.C. reflects the mind and interest of the royal court, its adminstrative personnel, and the powerful upper strata of society. What may be known of the lower classes comes either when they serve the court or rebel against it. In the complaint that his own peasants (*ḫupšu*) have left him, Rib-Addi of Byblos indirectly tells us of their extreme situation (*EA* 85:12ff.; 114:21ff.). Thus, in politically chaotic times of revolt such as that depicted in the Amarna period, one learns more of the people, their exploitation, and the defenders of the *status quo* than in court records of the royal family. It is the purpose of this study to examine the plight of the peasant during the Amarna Age in light of the remarks of the prominent anthropologist, Eric R. Wolf (1966). Thus, the further purpose of this paper will be to draw through inference conclusions on the role of the peasant in the social change in Canaan that underlay the emergence of the Israelites.

THE ARISTOCRACY

The form of society as found in the Ugaritic texts is that of a city-state kingdom. The king, although a vassal king of the Hittites, is the keystone of the social order; he enjoys the communion of the gods and men, and participates in the cult as high priest and mediator of divine revelation. With the aid of the gods and his own natural wisdom, he is the dispenser of justice to all his subjects. To guide him, communal custom replaces a codex of law. In times of war the king could lead his men in battle by reason of his personal charisma.

By the 14th century he waged war by means of a military aristocracy. In return for military service the king would grant parcels of land, some *in perpetuum* to his chariot warriors (*maryannu*-warrior), thus creating a relationship between himself and his barons that, for want of a better term, was "feudal." The military aristocracy, therefore, was composed of the chariot warriors, the commanders (*mru*), and the various other support groups of retainers, armorers, bowmen, etc. The royal household included not only a king and queen, but also their children—particularly the crown prince— brothers and sisters of the king, and various other relatives of the royal family. The palace personnel and its administrative staff composed the central government; there were senior executives (such as high minister

of the palace), royal commissioners of cities, diplomatic couriers, the entire
scribal school, and even merchants who were in the special employ of the
king. All of these together composed the aristocracy that appears in the
literature at Ugarit (Rainey 1962: 82–88).

Many members of the aristocracy, including the cult personnel,
received land grants in return for service rendered. Thus one might get land
through service to the king, either through cultic, administrative, or military
service; no provision was made in the text for anyone else nor any other
means, save revolt.

In the role of the ḫupšu, the peasant might be conscripted for compul-
sory labor for royal projects or armed services, possibly as a yeoman in the
infantry, or a bowman, or a reserve in general. The precise meaning of hpt
and its relation to ḫupšu is still a matter of continuing discussion. The
status of the hpt seems to be analogous to that of the maryannu; his
freedom from working the lands to render capital for the king was his "fief"
in perpetuum as much as land was that of the aristocratic maryannu; the
hpt was bound to render military service instead of agricultural quotas.
Yet, it is not incompatible that in times of peace he did work the land for
his own subsistence as the Alalakh texts suggest. The plight of the peasant
in the Amarna period was far more desperate than that seen in the Ugaritic
literature. Whatever tribal organization may have preceded the rise of the
feudal order, traces of it do not remain in the literature from Ugarit.

THE PEASANTRY

A study of the documents of the second millennium in Canaan depicts
a society which is anything but primitive. In a primitive society, producers
control the means of production, including their own labor, and they
exchange their own labor and its products for goods deemed culturally
necessary or for the service others may provide in return. This is certainly
not the case in a society based on feudal power as seen in Ugarit and in the
letters from Byblos. Such a primitive form is not apparent in Middle
Bronze Canaan; the control of the means of production, mainly human
labor, has passed from the individual to an executive group supported by
force. The king with his military aristocracy is the executive group ex-
ercising total control over the fund of power, the productivity of the
people, and their land.

In Mesopotamia, Egypt, and Canaan, the rulers used the surpluses
appropriated from the peasant group to underwrite their own standard of
living, distributing the remainder to non-agricultural groups, military and
cultic personnel, for specific goods and services. Goods were no longer
exchanged between groups but were first furnished to an administrative
center and only later redirected (Wolf 1964: 4).

Rib-Addi of Byblos informs the Pharaoh that his ḫupšu have pledged
as corvee their own sons and daughters (along with wooden implements for

cultivating the fields of Iarimuta) for deliverance of their lives (*EA* 81:33–41; 75:11–14; 74:15–17; 85:11–15; 90:36–39). If the Pharaoh does not give Rib-Addi grain to feed his peasants, they will desert him for his enemy, Abdi-Asirta (*EA* 85:8–15; 118:21–23; 125:14–30). Rib-Addi's own peasants have been advised to kill him because he has not provided for their safety and subsistence (*EA* 85:8–14). Finally, his own palace guard fails to protect him when attempted assassinations occur (*EA* 81:15–17; 74:25–26). The social balance has completely deteriorated from the serene description in the Keret Epic. In the Amarna period the subsistence level of the *ḫupšu* was not being met; this in turn signifies several other developments: (a) if the peasants do not have enough to eat, neither would he have enough surplus grain to provide seed for next year or to feed his own livestock; (b) if he has no way of replacing yearly tool loss (in fact, he has given them away to save his life), or (c) if he has no funds from which to carry on simple social relations such as a dowry for his daughter or a ceremonial offering for his family, or (d) if he is so destitute that he cannot pay his feudal taxes or rent for land use (since the kind or his grantee owns it), then he must seek an alternate way of survival (Wolf 1964: 7–9). Rib-Addi vividly states the stark reality that his peasants are joining the SA.GAZ men, the allies and confederates of his enemy Abdi-Asirta (*EA* 73:26; 74:19; 88:31–32; 84; 93; 138). He is well aware that, deprived of his peasants' fund of rent, he is deprived of his fund of power.

The texts from Ugarit and Amarna, reflecting the critical situation prevailing in Canaan during the 15th and 14th centuries, indicate that the *ḫupšu* had two possible strategies to follow to meet both the demands of the royal tax collectors and his household's sustenance. One, he might increase production, but this would depend on how he could manage the ingredients of production, namely, the land, his labor, and surplus (capital of some type); the data indicates that he had little possibility of going beyond or perhaps of meeting the minimal needs. Two, in politically chaotic times the traditional liens on his rent would have weakened because the central power structure has become ineffective (Wolf 1964: 15–16); therefore, he can escape the demands to underwrite payments and break traditional ties for religious support in three ways: (a) by claiming the land for himself in the face of no opposition, (b) by withdrawing from the old regime in favor of a stronger and more congenial one, or (c) by withdrawing from the land if he cannot succeed in any other manner. The recurrent phrase that "so and so" has joined the SA.GAZ in all probability signifies that they have defected their political allegiance by joining the "out-party."

Another alternative to the peasant, perhaps less dramatic but no less severe, would be to cut back to the bare necessities. Normally, this is the first line of action: he only eats basic items, makes minimal purchases, and relies upon home-grown produce as much as possible. In this precarious situation any novelty may upset the balance, and thus the peasant adheres to the traditional ways even more tenaciously. By nature, the peasant is not a joiner; the necessity of meeting the needs of staying alive without undue commitments to overlords explains his grassroots conservatism. In wartime, the urbanite may easily be separated from his livelihood, but the peasant has the land and his ability to make it yield. Thus it must be assumed that the Canaanite peasant of the Amarna period selected a path most convenient to his interest: for some, it would mean remaining faithful to the regent; for others, it was an opportunity to seize the land they worked; for yet others, it was time to revolt by joining those who stood over and against their oppressors.

The texts reflect that a network system of marketing was practiced in Canaan during the second millennium. In network markets there is a middleman, a professional, who stands between the primary producer and the consumer (Wolf 1964: 42). Thus a peasant might raise and sell his cattle to a merchant, who in turn, may market the milk, slaughter the cattle for beef, or sell the hides to the tanner. The peasant finds himself in a market in which prices are not governed by custom or kinship as in his rural village, but possibly by a stranger, or by impersonal laws of supply and demand that he may not entirely understand and which he certainly cannot control. In this form of competition the peasant must be prepared to sell many things— grain, milk, leather goods, even pots and pans if he has the skill—for whatever brings the best current market price. Between seeding and harvest the peasant may develop craft skills and products to be more flexible in meeting such a market. It is not inconceivable, therefore, that a peasant will also keep a herd of sheep, and a few cows and goats, and have a basic skill in tanning, weaving, or metalworking to meet survival needs. Because he has such limited resources in times of economic depression, during the short cycles of declining prices evident in periods of severe political chaos the peasant has few alternatives (Wolf 1964: 45). Times of political uncertainty are dangerous for the merchant as well as the peasant, but they afford chances for greater profiteering by the merchant. In such a crisis the peasant may decide to tend the crops himself and send his wife to sell and buy, or he may keep some male members at home for the fields and send his son and daughters out for hire as cited by Rib-Addi.

Caught in such economic binds, the peasant may confront the multiplication of middlemen by social exclusion, that is, grouping all specialists of a kind different from himself and his village as potential enemies. Thus he needs a social outlet through which he may cope with this economic domination. He very well may find that he is not alone in his misery, so a *cosa nostra* of peasants like himself may form; a mutual support relationship may develop but need not be lasting because its basis is not fundamental (Wolf 1964: 47). Local merchants such as smithies, leather workers, and scribes who practice discounts and "little extras" for favorite customers may be included. The peasant's enemy is anyone who has a claim on his fund of rent. This can be the merchant, the tax collector, the royal commissioner who sets the quotas and market prices, the labor contractor, and, ultimately, the king. They all have one interest in the peasant, namely, profit.

THE AXIS: LAND TENURE

In Canaan the land of the peasant belonged to the regent by right of domain, that is, the lord held ownership by heredity or royal grant for definite periods of time or forever. The regent would parcel lands to his peasants, grant hunting rights and rights to pasture, woodland and fuel. In return the peasant must pay in produce or labor. The peasant on his own level may furnish housing to landless laborers in return for their labor or sublease the land to tenant farmers. The lot of the slave or serf must have been that of the landless, possibly in the service of the free peasant. Although a case may be made that the *ḫupšu* were free proletarians, it would not take much stress on the system for the *ḫupšu* willingly (by reason of debt) or by force to become part of the slave population.

Rainey demonstrates from Ugaritic materials that the aristocracy held land in perpetuity; thus, land held through inheritance was based on kinship and carried with it the right to receive tribute from its peasants (Rainey 1962: 212–15). The Amarna texts reveal that the Pharaoh appointed chiefs of his Canaanite provinces to administer his realm in his stead. From the income derived from the peasants, the regents had a right to keep some of the taxes collected (and receive a salary from a central bureau as well). It afforded the king greater centralized control, because the regents depended upon his good will for their position. The feudal system was a two-edged sword: it was stable in its authority structure, but the landed aristocracy also provided a permanent power source of opposition to the king. Therefore, it was necessary to surround the lord-peasant relationship with ceremony to lessen the edge of the single interest, profit. In addition, ceremony relieved a constant anxiety of rulers everywhere: it underwrote their claim to legitimacy. Through ritual the regent may assume the power and glory of the gods or the absent Pharaoh by acting out myths of fertility for his peasants. Festivals give occasion for the normal state of the society to be put aside to ease the oppressive tension (Wolf 1964: 52). The Canaanites regulated the critical moments of life from birth to the grave by customs designed to separate the participants from historical time and place them for a period in mythical time.

DEBT TITLES

An in-depth study of the peasant's control of his land, water, seed, draft animals, tools, and labor is much needed to enable one to comprehend how his factors of production may and did become his "debt" titles. By the nature of their business, merchants could become creditors, money-lenders, and "bankers." A peasant may have to pay to enjoy water rights; if he has no money, he must borrow it and pay interest on his loan. The same may be true of his purchasing tools, and yet again, he may pay a rent for his draft animals. Thus, the creditor may keep the peasant permanently dependent at the lowest possible level (Wolf 1964: 55). If he deals in land and population density is heavy, the merchant may land-speculate and still create a competitive market for loans and mortgages. However, there is a danger: if he keeps the peasant at a minimum capacity for repayment, he then freezes capital. If the merchant cannot always and easily recover his loan (a bulk of laws indicate how real that possibility was), he will charge exorbitant interest rates of 50–75 percent.

One may cite as an illustration the case of chargeable rates of interest a money-lender might exact within the laws of Hammurabi. The relative value of the GUR, the basic monetary unit, was the basis for the rate of interest. Fluctuations of the GUR created fluctuations in the interest rate. But merchants recognized other rates as well: (1) "interest of the city" regulated by the town officials, (2) "interest of the market" fixed by the seller-group, (3) "interest of the temple" regulated by local temple priests, and (4) the "interest of Shamash" regulated by the royal temple at 20 percent. A money lender might exceed these rates depending on the instability of the government and the desperation of the debtor (cf. Driver and Miles 1952: 174; McKenzie 1965: 515; de Vaux 1961: 170–77).

At a time of political unrest there will be a steady turnover of those who hold claim to land and debt-titles. These short-term relations make for quick money situations and increased tensions between the impoverished peasant and the merchant group. An existence of a class of landlords and money-lenders, whose real interests lie in living in urban areas removed from the countryside and who at the same time, are aspiring for political office or favor, as well as, exploiting the rural opportunity as a means of accumulating wealth to further their social climbing, creates an explosive moment in time. The city benefits from the surplus milked from the countryside by the urban rent collectors without generating further work-incentive for the peasant. This system is self-limiting because it reduces the rewards by lowering the peasant's existence to a bare minimum (Wolf 1964: 56).

Caution must be used regarding the shift in the semantic range of ḫupšu in texts that span the period from early to late second millennium, that is, texts from Babylon, Nuzi, Alalakh, Ugarit, Amarna, and even as late as 1 Sam 17:25. From the Amarna usage it would be difficult to press the case that the ḫupšu were landless peasants, or free proletarians, or tenant farmers. It is apparent that they were economically and legally bound to their regent, the city-state ruler appointed by Egypt. What is of immediate interest to us is their relationship to the group termed the SA.GAZ people.

FROM PEASANTS TO SA.GAZ

It has been convincingly argued by Moshe Greenberg (1955: 85–88) that the SA.GAZ of the 2 millennium were an ethnically heterogeneous class of people found in Mesopotamia, Syria, and Palestine. Within the successive ethnic movements of various peoples during the period, there continued to be a social class of indigent, restless peoples mixed with the settled populations. Once the social and political chaos diminished at the end of the millennium, they seemed to disappear as well. Yet even during the centuries of intense tribal migrations, the SA.GAZ can be seen to be an element of the settled rather than the nomadic population. Nearly without exception cities and countries were given as their place of origin. They had special quarters in the city of Aleppo; they were given a city by Amanhatbi of Tusulti (*EA* 185; 186); even when they were accused of plundering and burning the cities, their base of operations was not the desert but a city.

The use of the term seems to indicate that one would not wish to be called a SA.GAZ by one's friend. Rival city heads, such as Shuwardata (Keilah is one of his cities), Milkilu of Gezer, and Abdi-Heba of Jerusalem, are at various times allied with one another against the third member (*EA* 280; 290a; 289; 271). Throughout the shifting alliance they consistently regard their opponent as the SA.GAZ. To be hostile to Rib-Addi of Gubla (Byblos) is to become like the SA.GAZ. A difficulty with the Amarna usage is that while in the main the term SA.GAZ is used in a pejorative sense, it is not true in every instance. However, in the mind of Rib-Addi, who can bring no specific charge against Abdi-Asirta or Aziru, the term is charged with the implication of political sedition.

Rib-Addi was unable to convince the Pharaoh that his empire was virtually lost because of the hostility of the SA.GAZ people. There were no hordes invading from the desert to seize the cities; there was only a change in political control of the city-states, a change which the Pharaoh did not think worth the bother as long as he continued to receive tribute. It was through political intrigue, intimidation, and bribery that the SA.GAZ gained control of a city and its territory. Harrassment of the peasants prevented the harvesting of crops, and the fields were abandoned. All forms of peasant economy, even the simple sheep herding, were shut down. Edward F. Campbell (1965: 193, n. 3) notes that Biridiya's scribe often implied by "harvest" the meaning: "We were not able to pluck the wool." The peasants would not survive if they remained loyal to the regent; the alternative was to join the SA.GAZ. Such harassment was the common practice for Abdi-Asirta, Aziru, Labaya. Thus, Rib-Addi pleaded that (1) law and order could no longer be maintained; (2) his enemies derived their power from the lawless, rebellious element; and (3) even the Pharaoh's regents were joining them.

It is immediately apparent that the SA.GAZ were considered socially inferior. They were dependent and landless. They were outside their original social group, whether by choice or not; they enjoyed no legal status within the feudal system. They took what they could get. In this context Rib-Addi's constant reference to Abdi-Asirta as a stray dog is socially apropos. But to live totally unattached would invite extinction, so some adherence to another political authority must be expected. This out-group would differ from the in-group only because of their new legal and political status. The mistaken notion that all SA.GAZ were impoverished must be avoided. If one recalls that the regents and members of the military aristocracy became SA.GAZ, then one should not expect that all were impoverished or nomadic. Any dissident could be a SA.GAZ-man. And although Abdi-Asirta and his son, Aziru, were strong rulers in the eyes of Egypt, they could very well be SA.GAZ in the view of Rib-Addi, for they stood outside the normal political policy of one regency respecting another.

George Mendenhall (1973: 131–35) reasons that there are three basic constituents in the term SA.GAZ: (1) loss of status: one must be ejected, have fled or withdrawn from a previous group; (2) two-fold loss of status in a legal-political community: (a) the SA. GAZ no longer feel bound by the customary legal obligations, "they do as they please," and (b) they are no longer enjoying the protection and privileges of the society; only force can deal with them; and (3) they are said to use illegitimate force against the demands of the existing political structure.

FROM SA.GAZ TO ISRAELITES

Despite the major political disturbances in Canaan during the Middle Bronze Age, the cultural tradition remains fundamentally continuous. However, a general deterioration in physical culture occurs between 1500 and 1100 B.C. The upheaval between 1250 and 1150 B.C. reaches from Alalakh to Lachish in which many cities were destroyed—many were rebuilt but not immediately nor along the same lines. Al Glock (1970: 583) sees three reasons promoting the political disturbances: (1) Philistines, Sea-Peoples, and "Hebrews" were moving in; (2) *Habiru* and peasants were revolting against social, political and economic conditions in Canaanite life; and finally (3) Egypt was unable to keep pace with city-state intrigue. This is the approximate historical setting for the appearance of the new people in Canaan, the Israelites.

It may be projected that the political turmoil witnessed in the Amarna letters did not conclude with the last datable tablet, but continued piecemeal until the unification of the land by David. In Canaan during the 14th century defection from the political rule, in the form of cities and lands joining the SA.GAZ, included members from every class of society. For revolt, a common cause was needed. In times of political stress—as the Amarna letters portray—the opportunity was present for peasants to form coalitions. A major difference in the Amarna document and those of early Israel is the lack of tribal consciousness in the early 14th century and the marked awareness of it in the subsequent period of the Judges. A social and political transformation had occurred during the hiatus.

Seti I, Ramses II, and Merneptah attempted to reassert effective political domination in Canaan following the Amarna period. Their limited successes at Beth-shan, Kadesh and Shechem, and their withdrawal subsequent to the arrival of the Sea-Peoples leaves considerable room for local developments. It is the conviction of this writer that a significant number of the peasants had formed coalitions led by dissident regents and members of the military aristocracy. The temporal coincidence of the Israelite settlement and the politically ripe conditions for a peasant coalition are too great to be ignored. It is not necessary that such a political process—that is, peasant coalition overcoming a city-state system—be a violent one. But it is possible that in small and sporadic ways it was a violent process. Two factors in a peasant-based revolt should be recalled: (1) the peasants' tendency toward autonomy, and (2) an equally strong tendency to form coalitions on a more or less unstable basis for short-range ends (Wolf 1964: 91–92). It may not be difficult to arouse a peasant group to common action, but it is quite difficult to maintain unity both while in action and after the short-term goal is achieved. Thus, for lack of a catalyst, local periodic eruptions might continue over a long period of time without uniting into a major force. Such a projection might be explained in those terms for that period in history between the end of the Amarna letters and the time of the emergence of the Israelites as a dominant group in Canaan.

Racial distinction is a relatively modern notion that has come about since the rise of nationalism. In ancient Canaan the basic unit was the family associated with other families in a village; a cluster of families may constitute a clan with its village center. Several clans would comprise a tribe with a territorial center in some major city within its boundaries. Clearly, a tribe would not necessarily be a racially pure group but simply an administrative unit within a federation of tribes. Albrecht Alt may be quite accurate in his concept that what had transpired was a change in political and social structure from the city-state to tribal, but not one from a racially diverse population associated with cosmopolitan urban centers to a racially pure population which entered from the uninhabitable areas of the desert. The emergence then of the Israelites as a dominant group in the late Bronze Age should not be considered so much an incursion of new peoples from outside of Canaan but rather the emergence of the peasants of Canaan within the land. The analysis of the role of the peasant, a native Canaanite, presented here differs from the view of Jean Dus (1975) who reasons that Joshua led a revolt of Palestinian Hebrew slaves against the city-state rulers. These Hebrews were Habiru-SA.GAZ peoples that had peacefully wandered into Canaan and had been enslaved by the Canaanites.

It would seem to this writer that this anaylsis provides a conceptual model for understanding the social and political milieu out of which the Israelites rose. Only in part does it explain the early Israelite rejection of

kingship. At Shechem, Joshua issues a "call to arms." The predominant
feature of this covenant is the choice the people are to make: (a) serve the
ancestral gods of a former homeland "beyond the River," (b) serve the
native gods of Canaan, or (c) serve Yahweh, the author of the mighty acts
related in Josh 24:1–13. The exclusive allegiance to Yahweh precludes
loyalty to any other deity, even deities represented by human kings.

The Israelite movement was a radical rejection of the divinity of any
human ruler. It proclaimed Yahweh as lord of the land, as judge, and as
warrior: all functions claimed by the Canaanite aristocracy. At a certain
moment, not yet well determined, the Canaanite peasant coalition was fired
by the historical precedent of a people freed by Yahweh from the immediate
control of the Pharaoh in Egypt. The new society replaced city-state feudalism with tribal confederacy, the privileged relationship of the king to the
gods with each follower enjoying access to Yahweh, the monopoly of the
land by the special few with each believer as a tenant of Yahweh, and the
social stratification according to wealth with a society "that depended
entirely on its demonstrated value to human beings— and its willingness to
remain within the ethical bonds to which *all* members of the community
were obligated" (Mendenhall 1973: 195).

BIBLIOGRAPHY

Campbell, E. F.
    1965   Shechem in the Amarna Archives. Appendix 2, pp. 191–207 in *Shechem: The
            Bibliography of a Biblical City*, G. E. Wright. New York: McGraw-Hill.
Driver, G. R., and Miles, J. C., eds.
    1952   *The Babylonian Laws*. Oxford: Clarendon.
Dus, J.
    1975   Moses or Joshua? On the Problem of the Founder of the Israelite Religion.
            Radical Religion 2:26–41.
EA =
            Die El-Amarna-tafeln. J. A. Knudtzon, Leipzig: J. C. Hinrichs. 1908–15.
Glock, A.
    1970   Early Israel as the Kingdom of Israel. *Concordia Theological Monthly* 41: 558–
            605.
Greenberg, M.
    1955   *The Hab/piru*. American Oriental Series 39, eds. H. M. Hoenigswald, J.
            DeFrancis, G. Mendenhall. New Haven: American Oriental Society.
McKenzie, J. L.
    1965   Loans. Pp. 515–16 in *Dictionary of the Bible*. London/Dublin: G. Chapman.
Mendenhall, G.
    1973   *The Tenth Generation*. Baltimore: Johns Hopkins.
Rainey, A.
    1962   *The Social Stratification of Ugarit*. Unpublished Ph.D. dissertation, Brandeis
            University.
Vaux, R. de
    1961   *Ancient Israel*. Trans. J. McHugh. New York: McGraw-Hill.
Wolf, E.
    1966   *Peasants*. Englewood Cliffs: Prentice-Hall.

Early Israel and the Canaanite
Socio-economic System*

Norman K. Gottwald

In recent years the hypothesis has been advanced that early Israel originated in a socio-economic and religio-political revolution among native Canaanites of the lower and disprivileged classes (Mendenhall 1962, 1973; Gottwald 1974, 1975, 1976, 1978, 1979). To sustain this argument for an Israelite peasant revolution against the Canaanite city-state rulers, it is necessary to determine not only the political economy of premonarchic Israel but also the political economy of ancient Canaan. This study attempts to make a start on the latter project.

CANAANITE "FEUDALISM"?

Feudalism is a political and economic system based on the relationship between lord and vassal which results from land being held by the vassal on condition of homage and service to the lord. The term is often reserved for Europe from the 9th through the 15th centuries, related developments elsewhere being characterized as "feudal tendencies."

With some misgivings, scholars have generally treated Canaanite society as "feudal" in type or as "quasi-feudal," i.e., resembling feudalism, or "semi-feudal," i.e., partially feudal. This is an appealing interpretation *politically* because of the small political units in Canaan which were engaged in military competition fostered by a chariot-warrior class. It is appealing *economically* because a majority of the populace was locked into a mode of agricultural production wherein the ruling class took the surplus and at will commanded the labor force in periodic corveé.

It is problematic, however, whether such loose descriptions are specific to feudalism. The precisely formulated land-tenure ties and personal relations between noblemen and serfs, so abundantly documented in medieval Europe, are not clearly evident in Canaan. This omission seems to arise not merely from a gap in the legal documents from Canaan, since the diplomatic and administrative texts that touch upon relationships between the rulers and the ruled do not describe ties that are closely analogous to those in European feudalism. Still more problematic is the heightening of state authority in Syro-Palestine and the expansion of trade evident in the Amarna Age. These developments were precisely opposite to those ac-

---

*Revision of "Early Israel and 'the Asiatic Mode of Production' in Canaan," *Society of Biblical Literature 1976 Seminar Papers*, ed. G. MacRae, Missoula: Scholars Press, 145-54.

companying the rise of feudalism in Europe, which followed the breakdown of political empires and the decline of trade.

Most scholars agree that Canaanite ḫupšu were peasants, but were they feudal peasants, i.e., serfs? The problem is illustrated by the differing interpretations of William F. Albright (1926, 1936) and Isaac Mendelsohn (1941, 1955). Albright chose to call the ḫupšu, "serfs," whereas Mendelsohn preferred to see them as "free proletarians" comparable to the *coloni*, "tied tenant farmers," of the Roman Empire. More recently, M. Heltzer (1969) and H. Klengel (1969) have argued that ḫupšu were a group of court clients, "royal men," who owed various "service duties" to the king, duties which were mainly military though some pertained to crafts and professions. These scholars doubt that feudalism is the best model for understanding Syro-Palestinian social organization, but they do not propose an alternative model. None of these discussions proceeds on a broad enough basis to address fundamentally the question of the political economy of ancient Canaan.

MARX'S "ASIATIC MODE OF PRODUCTION"

An alternative to the feudal model for ancient Asia is the notion of an "Asiatic mode of production." Conceptions of "oriental" or "Asiatic" society have circulated since the 17th century and were particularly stressed by Montesquieu and Hegel. Marx and Engels worked out a more precise theory of the Asiatic mode of production in the 1850's under three primary influences: (1) the economists John Stuart Mill and Richard Jones; (2) accounts of travels, memoirs, and monographs on Eastern countries; and (3) studies Marx made of village communities in Scotland and Spain.

Marx noted that when British capitalism penetrated China and India, it found intact a traditional form of political economy that had persisted from antiquity. He concluded that China and India— together with ancient Egypt, Mesopotamia, and Islamic societies—had followed an essentially different route of political economy than had Europe. Europe had followed the progression from primitive communism (e.g., Celtic, Nordic, and Teutonic tribes) through slavery (Greek city-states and the Roman Empire) and feudalism (landed nobility and serfs in the Middle Ages) to capitalism (urban trade and industrialism based on private ownership of the means of production replacing craft guilds). In Asia, on the other hand, Marx concluded that in the place of slavery and feudalism there existed a variant type of class society determined by distinctive environmental and sociohistorical factors. In this century more sophisticated analyses of the Asiatic mode of production have been offered for China (Wittfogel 1931), India (Kosambi 1956) and Islam (Rodinson 1966).

In the Asiatic mode of production a contrast is drawn between the simple *village community* as the locus of production and the highly developed and powerful *centralized state*. The interaction of these two socio-economic and political units creates the peculiarities of this mode of production.

Primary wealth is in land, and it is held communally according to kin and village social structures that tend to persist in spite of changes in political regimes. Farming and crafts are closely associated in the village community. The products of field and herd, as well as crafted articles, are chiefly for immediate use by the producers rather than for an exchange market. There is simple barter among the producers on a small scale.

Over against the relatively self-contained productive units in the villages stands the central authority of the state. The geographic and climatic necessity of large-scale waterworks for irrigation and flood control probably had much to do with facilitating the growth of the state as a reliable means for building, repairing, and operating these waterworks. The state functioned not only economically but also politically. It developed powerful ruling groups which took large shares of the village economic surplus to build palaces, fortifications and temples, to equip armies, and to provide luxurious living for the privileged. Under the auspices of the state, there arose privileged social strata, such as large landholders, merchants, and bankers. They had the means to seize and to channel village wealth by concentrating fields and flocks under their control and by converting landed wealth into profitable trade.

The interaction of village and state was not conducive to technological change and economic growth. The cities as administrative centers of the state could penetrate the villages and confiscate their economic surpluses for state-approved uses. However, the city itself, was not a major independent source of wealth; it lived on the countryside. Although the new social strata of privilege had enormous advantages in the use of the wealth taken from the villages, they were decisively held in check by the political rulers. They did not find a way to encourage technological improvement, to facilitate "modernizing" social change in the villages, or to "rationalize" the economy as a whole.

As a result, the village did not throw off state control in any lasting way although there were repeated peasant uprisings; yet the city did not break up or replace the village as the basic socio-economic productive unit, although it constantly invaded the village and drained off its wealth.

State-protected merchants became wealthy, but trade and crafts for the exchange market functioned chiefly on the international frontiers. Political rulers and privileged social strata were the main beneficiaries of this lucrative trade, while the great majority of people remained on the land and made or bartered the necessary articles of daily life.

Thus, the Asiatic mode of production was characterized by vast populaces living on communally held land that was worked at a low technological level, while a politically controlling minority operated the

extensive waterworks and directed the village surpluses into state projects
and into the enrichment of privileged landholders and merchants.

In some respects this Asiatic mode of production looks like feudalism.
Labor services and heavy rent or mortgage payments are imposed on
peasants. The produce of the land tends to be monopolized by an
advantaged minority. However, the political units are larger and more
powerful than those of European feudalism. The absentee owners have
questionable legal entitlement to the land they hold, and they are not
personally bound to the peasants as in the nobleman/serf ties of feudalism.
Trade is thriving but under state sponsorship or regulation and with little
effect on the masses of people. The enterprising social strata do not
compose the ruling class but are held in check on the one hand by the
peasants and on the other by the state.

THE ENTERPRISING STATE AND THE VILLAGE COMMUNITY IN CANAAN

What light does this hypothesis of an Asiatic mode of production
throw on ancient Canaanite political economy and on the origins of Israel?
What elements of Syro-Palestinian socio-economics and politics are com-
patible with the hypothesis? What elements are neutral or ambiguous?
What elements are resistant or contrary? What data are we lacking to be
able to form a judgment? What data may be available but previously
overlooked?

Without pretending to completeness, I shall indicate some lines of
analysis and reflection.

1) On Centralized Waterworks as the Basis of Political Economy

Wittfogel's study (1931) of the Chinese version of Asiatic irrigation
societies has been taken up by several students of ancient Near Eastern
society with varying degrees of interest and approval (Harris 1968: 671-87;
Adams 1966). Many believe that the enormous task of taking full advantage
of the waters of the Nile and the Tigris-Euphrates had much to do with an
early development of strong states in those regions. Other observers have
called attention to additional factors which may have been as important, or
more important, in the development of the Near Eastern state: supervision
of crop rotation; cultivation and security of the fields; military protection
of the villages; development of labor-intensive crafts, such as mining and
metallurgy; population growth; the multiplicity of subsistence pursuits,
resulting in trade and other redistributive mechanisms; etc. Possibly the
original, fundamental need to construct and maintain extensive waterworks
instigated the growth of the centralized state in the Near East, but
additional factors (noted above) contributed to its development and molded
it in certain directions.

More specifically, was irrigation/flood control the basis of the state in
Canaan, since that region lacked the massive waterworks of the Nile or of

the Tigris-Euphrates? First, it needs to be recognized that a larger amount of small-scale irrigation existed in ancient Canaan than is generally conceded. Recent archeological work devoted to exploring the irrigation and terrace systems in the Israelite highlands suggests that locally developed water systems (like the apparently ancient installations at Jerusalem and in the vicinity of Bethlehem) probably had a lot to do with the successful Israelite agricultural settlements (De Geus 1975; Wilkinson 1974). In addition, marsh drainage, dikes, and canals would have been significant projects for communities along the upper reaches of the Jordan River and in the vicinity of coastal streams such as the Yarkon and Kishon. Research on these water systems as functional wholes, rather than as isolated urban water tunnels and pools, is just beginning in a disciplined way.

Nonetheless, had the entire Near Eastern water supply consisted of such small rivers and streams and such localized highland springs, it is doubtful that the state would have been needed to take over water control from the village communities. Thus, the phenomenon of the powerful, enterprising state in Syro-Palestine may be explained by the region's strategic importance as a corridor between the major river valleys. This situation created pressure on strong states at both poles to reproduce their governmental forms throughout the corridor in order to control it or, more indirectly, to stimulate the formation of states by peoples of the corridor in defensive response.

From at least Hyksos times—five centuries before the rise of Israel—the impact of imperial politics from the Nile, the Tigris-Euphrates, and Anatolia led to diffusion of the dominant, enterprising state within the Syro-Palestinian corridor. Given the topography and modest irrigation possibilities, the central authorities which developed in Canaan were generally small in scale, composed usually of a fortified administrative center with satellite towns and villages in a supportive rural hinterland. We conventionally speak of these Canaanite political entities as "city-states," but probably we do so largely with reference to their scale rather than on the basis of an accurate assessment of their internal organization. For example, ancient Near Eastern "primitive democracy," of which Jacobsen (1943) has written, may be far less analogous to Greek city-states than to vestiges of village community organization not wholly stamped out within towns that served as administrative centers.

(2) On the Social Structure of Canaanite States and the Social Structure of Early Israel

The hypothesis of an Asiatic mode of production offers intriguing possibilities for further research and theorizing. The old assumption that ancient Canaan was a feudal society makes it difficult to explain the village and tribal base of the Israelite social movement. As long as the Israelites were assumed to have been pastoral nomads, this was, of course, hardly a matter calling for explanation. It was taken for granted that, as culturally simple pastoral nomads, the Israelites were perforce tribal. With the dawning realization that pastoral nomadism was no more than a minor component in ancient Israel and, in any event, was well integrated into settled life (Gottwald 1974, 1979), the village-based tribalism of early Israel calls for fundamental reexamination.

It is difficult, for example, to trace social-organizational continuity from the tribes of Gaul and Germany to the life of European feudal estates. The old communal forms of property holding were long dissolved in the lord's unchallenged status as owner of the manor and in the serf's dependence on the lord. If the Israelites did not bring tribalism and notions of communal land holding with them from the desert, where did they get this form of social organization? The hypothesis of the Asiatic mode of production suggests that the cohesive village community had *not been stamped out*. To be sure, the village community had been *imposed upon* by central authorities, threatening the independent life of the peasants by a credit and loan system that threw them into practical bondage to absentee creditors and by periodic levies of goods and services demanded of the peasants as the price of economic and military "security." Still, the traditional pattern of communal land tenure was not, it seems, legally abolished, and neither advancing technology nor a grass-roots exchange market arose to break up the village social structures in favor of a new social order. The careerist and client groups around the court and the international exchange market persisted as an alien overlay on the equally persistent, tribally oriented village.

Viewed in this way, the Israelite tribes may be conceived as a "revitalization" or "retribalization" movement (Gottwald 1975; 1979: 323–28, 697–700). What was decisively different about Israel was that it constituted a very broad alliance of extended families, protective associations, and tribes that managed to throw off the central authorities and take over formerly state-operated socio-economic, military, and religious functions at the village and tribal levels (Gottwald, 1979, Parts VI-VII). In this model, everything depended on the Israelite revolutionary movement attaining *a sufficient scale and sophistication of coordination* to provide the basic services that the central authority had claimed as its prerogatives. In particular, the Israelite movement had to defend itself against the counter-revolutionary thrusts of the ousted authorities. One of the political ploys of these authorities was to keep villages divided from one another and incapable of combination for united counteraction against the state. In Canaan, with Egyptian imperial influence weakened, the Israelites faced a multiplicity of these small states. The Israelite success lay in uniting villages along tribal organizational lines until the movement spilled over former state boundaries and spread a new political economy over an area and among a populace many times larger than the area, or populace, of anyone of the resisting city-states.

If other Asiatic societies are any index, it is likely that more peasant uprisings occurred in the ancient Near East—and in Canaan—than the records of the central authorities report. What seems to have characterized most of these peasant uprisings under the Asiatic mode of production was a rapid return to state authority as new dynasties were installed by, or taken over from, the rebels. It appears to have been a peculiarity of Israel that it sustained its nonauthoritarian organizational thrust for some two centuries, persistently leveling all attempts to constitute a new central authority until it had to deal more concertedly with the stepped-up Philistine threat. The Philistines posed a level of hostile state power and militarism which Israel could only combat by resorting to a strong military chiefdom which culminated in the dynasty of David and Solomon.

In this way the old conflict between the village community and the enterprising state intruded into the Israelite community itself—but with a difference. The difference was that the Israelite state faced extraordinary obstacles to its enlargement and restraints on its power precisely because its village communities were not isolated units but had developed networks of self-rule and self-service. The village-tribal ethos and religion had been so well cultivated during Israel's first two centuries that it was this "lower" level of social organization that tended to shape the national culture and to stamp the religion as a persistent critical force against the state. The model of the Asiatic mode of production suggests that we need a more careful inquiry into the division of labor between the Israelite state and the Israelite village tribal networks in the various periods of monarchic history in both Israelite kingdoms as well as in the united monarchy.

THE VIABILITY OF THE VILLAGE COMMUNITY IN CANAAN

Is it at all reasonable to suppose that in Canaan communal property holdings in villages—and the accompanying socio-economic organization—could have survived close to two millennia of pressure from state power and at least half a millennium of the more highly bureaucratized and militarized state that took root with the Hyksos? Would not the heavy hand of state taxation in kind, impressment of the peasantry into army and labor service, onerous loans at interest, merchant profiteering, and famines, wars, and migrations have completely destroyed the village commune in the course of a few centuries?

One answer is certainly that the tendency of state-sponsored trade to convert the village community's use values into exchange values did not go unchallenged. We hear enough about pressure for social justice, periodic reforms, and overthrown dynasties to know that the village community possessed sufficient socio-economic productivity, political resistance, and overall resiliency to "spring back" from the repeated incursions of land-owning, merchant, and banking classes. Israel's vigorous coalition of village communities was doubtless only the most striking instance of the general tendency of those communities to put up resistance to the predatory social strata sponsored by the state.

It is probable that the tenacity and viability of tribally organized villages varied markedly throughout Canaan. Villages close to administrative centers, and most affected by international trade, would have been least likely to maintain tribal traditions and practices. More distant villages, especially those in the thicketed uplands, would have been most likely to maintain an enduring tribal mode of existence. It is noteworthy that it was in the upland region that the Israelite movement first got its hold in Canaan. This was facilitated both by the terrain, which was favorable to guerilla warfare, and by the readiness of the local populace to opt out of the city-state system.

Also of great moment to the viability of the village community was the nature of the ideology or intellectual culture that was dominant. Much of our information about the history of ideas in Canaan comes to us from texts and artifacts that belonged to the political rulers or their clients. Only in the literature of early Israel do we directly hear the voices of the disprivileged peoples of Canaan. However, when we do learn of peasant uprisings in Asiatic societies, they often are fueled by particular ideologies— frequently religious in nature—which serve to mark them off from the ruling ideas among the political elites they are opposing.

Students of ancient Near Eastern societies have not pursued adequately the class bias of the ideas expressed in the political and religious texts that have survived. Specifically, there is a tendency to assume that the points of view and the religio-political symbols found in the texts were shared widely and evenly throughout the society. We do not have much information, for example, on whether Canaanite mythology was the same at the grassroots as it was among the political elite and, in particular, whether village folk were as ready to grant religious validation to the state as were those who wrote the religious texts known to us.

In fact, a still unanswered question is the extent to which the ideologies of the ancient Near Eastern centralized states succeeded in creating popular cultures that cemented the populace in a common world view. Is it possible that we assume naively the same level and breadth of ideological cohesion for these ancient ideologies that we do for later historical religions such as Judaism, Christianity, Islam, Hinduism, and Buddhism? For example, did the religio-political ideology of ancient Canaan penetrate the whole society to the extent that Christian theocratic ideology penetrated the ethos of European feudalism? It is possible that the village community in Canaan could survive in part because of its relative imperviousness to the theocratic ideology that validated the state.

Effective resistance to a dominant ideology requires a counter ideology which can unite restive peoples. Sometimes this may be composed of elements of folk religion and folklore that invest land and family with supportive meanings which serve as defensive protection against domination from outside. Still more effective is an ideology that overarches immediate local concerns, uniting people on a broad basis in direct opposition to the ruling ideology. Israelite religion offered just such a broad and sharply combative ideology that gathered rebellious villagers under its banner against the state in the name of a newly active deity who invested disprivileged peoples with historic meaning.

In this section we are enlarging on the earlier claim that the village community could survive because the apparently powerful state, although exerting power over the village community and expropriating its wealth, did not develop the means to alter it fundamentally—socially, economically, or culturally. In the later Roman Empire, rural communities declined considerably so that slavery increased enormously and a "free" urban proletariat arose. Still more dramatic and far-reaching was the impact of trade and industrial technology in Europe, especially after capitalism took root, so that land enclosure, inflated rent charges, and the factory system threw a majority of the populace off the land and expelled them from the old craft-guild system of manufacture. By contrast, private capital on a large scale did not develop in the ancient Near East. There was neither the same mass exodus from the land nor the technological means to mass produce for an indefinitely expanding market. In the hands of central authority, a lucrative surplus in kind and in labor was extracted from the village communities for immediate use and for exchange of luxury goods by the privileged classes, for state sectors of the economy (such as mining), for monumental construction, and for military goods and services. But as a whole, state and village communities stalemated one another, and the forms of new wealth created by the state were held in check; thus, the stagnancy of this mode of production and the persisting traditionalism of the village.

ON TESTING AND APPLYING THE ASIATIC MODEL IN CANAAN

If feudalism is no longer the appropriate model for thinking about society and economy in ancient Canaan, we may have new ways for understanding the role of various social groupings reported in the Syro-Palestinian texts. Two examples may be cited.

The "military aristocrats" (*maryannu*) have been reevaluated of late in ways that appear to question their feudal standing as propertied, independent lords. H. Reviv (1972), for example, finds that dynasts, growing fearful of a concentration of power in the hands of a charioteer military caste, began to appoint *maryannu* aristocrats to civilian posts and to draw lower class elements into the charioteer ranks, a move that tended to sever military performance from the independent wealth otherwise requisite to provide and maintain costly military equipment. M. Heltzer (1969) goes further by denying that the *maryannu* ever were privileged aristocrats. In his view they were, like the *ḫupšu*, royal servants who owed service-duties, lived on royal land held conditionally, and received all their arms and equipment from royal stores.

As for the much-discussed ᶜapiru (often associated with biblical "Hebrews"), they may perhaps be viewed—as Jankowska (1969) proposed, although her evidence is based mainly on Nuzi—not so much as individual free-floating rebels or refugees but as groups of people pushed out of the security system of the family communes or village communities as a consequence of increasingly specialized production (e.g., specialized production of fruits and vegetables in agriculture and handcrafts for trade). The ᶜapiru may be viewed as a supplementary labor force which showed a tendency toward improvisation in socio-economic organization by adapting aspects of village community structure to occupational band, or guild, formations. Assuming that the ᶜapiru formed a sizable element in early Israel, it is probable that their organizational and military experience counted heavily in teaching other Israelites (especially peasants and pastoral nomads) how to cope with central authorities across previously constricting geographical, socio-economic, and political boundaries.

Obviously, our lack of law codes from Egypt and Syro-Palestine seriously handicaps efforts at more exact probes and testings of the hypothesis of an Asiatic mode of production in those regions. We can, however, go back to a fresh appraisal of the Mesopotamian and Hittite codes and of the administrative and diplomatic documents from Syro-Palestine. It is hoped that the recent archival finds at ancient Ebla in Syria may have something significant to tell us on these matters. These extra-biblical probes will, in any case, stimulate renewed attention to the biblical materials themselves and to the long-neglected potentialities of historical and cultural material strategies in archeology, which have proven productive in American Indian studies—in fact, productive almost everywhere else except in biblical archeology with its dominant orientation toward literary and directly historical interests.

One reason that the inquiry into ancient Canaanite political economy has been so imprecise is scholarly unawareness that we are in fact talking about two separate but closely interrelated realities: first, the actual physical means and the forms of social cooperation by which production was carried out, and second, the social, political, and legal relationships and mechanisms by which the products were allocated to the various groups of producers and nonproducers. Both the structure of production and the allocation of goods and services contain complex elements that are further complicated by particular mixtures of the two structures which differ according to time and place.

Eric R. Wolf (1966) analyzes (1) the different ways peasants produce in various ecotypes and (2) the different forms employed by ruling non-producers in their appropriation of peasant surpluses. He cautions that the right of domain, i.e., the right to command wealth from peasant land need not be based on private ownership. He distinguishes three basic types of domain over peasants: (1) patrimonial domain (sometimes called feudal), wherein rights to receive goods and services from the occupants of land are inherited; (2) prebendal domain, wherein rights to goods and services are noninherited grants attached to state offices or services to the state; (3) mercantile domain, wherein land becomes private property which can be bought and sold at profit, as well as borrowed against, and on which rent can be collected. Wolf observes that prebendal domain is especially common in strongly centralized bureaucratic states, notably in Asia, and that the prebends occur in the form of direct variable income from land or in the form of tax farming rights or fixed salary from land. He further notes that both patrimonial and prebendal domain are likely to be surrounded with ceremonial activities incumbent on lord and peasant. This ceremony has the effect of softening the impact of domain on the peasants and of legitimating the role of the lord. Domain ceremony, which often includes the notion that the lords are representatives or servants of the deity, is obviously another way of looking at the issue of ideology as discussed above.

Particularly pertinent to our inquiry is Wolf's conclusion that these forms of domain are not mutually exclusive but frequently appear in combination in a socio-economic formation. In medieval Europe north of the Alps, patrimonial domain was dominant, but with an admixture of prebendal grants to secular and ecclesiastical lords; moreover, ways were found to transfer patrimonial rights from one person to another. Of course, from the 13th century on, mercantile domain increased until it totally replaced the other forms of domain. For our purposes, Wolf's characterization of the domain mix in the East is provocative. Prebendal domain was dominant there, but nonetheless, "there were always periods and places where prebendal lords were able, either legally or illegally, to render their official domains heritable and/or marketable" (1966:54).

These observations of Wolf should cause us to challenge any lingering assumptions about a monolithic Canaanite political economy. Past interpreters of Canaanite economy tended to see *only* a patrimonial or feudal form of domain over the peasantry. In shifting toward another model, along the lines of the Asiatic mode of production, we easily could fall into the trap of claiming *only* a prebendal or noninheritable/ nonmarketable state grant of domain in ancient Canaan. At least such a prebendal monopoly ought not to be posited in advance. Wolf's analysis should open up the possibility that contradictory data in biblical and extrabiblical sources in fact may reflect different coexisting legal forms of domain and their attendant socio-political forms. To be sure, this will not allow us intellectual sloppiness in assuming an incoherent patchwork of domains. Doubtless one form, probably the prebendal, will be seen to dominate and to serve as a decisive point of departure in shaping the more atypical patrimonial and mercantile exceptions. By combining an awareness of mixed coexistent domains with an awareness of temporal development and regional peculiarities in the domain mixtures, we will be in a better methodological position to evaluate the socio-economic data on ancient Canaan. The same readiness to admit mixed domains may also be highly relevant to our efforts to understand more precisely the reemergence of domains over the peasantry in monarchic Israel once the founding peasant revolution had abated and the state officials and clients moved to reassert the ancient "right" of elites to control the rural cultivators.

BIBLIOGRAPHY

Adams, R. M.
  1966   *The Evolution of Urban Society: Early Mesopotamia and Prehispanic Mexico.* Chicago: Aldine.
Albright, W. F.
  1926   Canaanite ḥapši and Hebrew ḥofši. *Journal of the Palestine Oriental Society* 6: 107.
  1936   New Canaanite Historical and Mythological Data. *Bulletin of the American Schools of Oriental Research* 63: 23–32.
Coulborn, R., ed.
  1965   *Feudalism in History.* Princeton, NJ: Princeton.
Geus, C. H. J. de
  1975   The Importance of Archaeological Research into the Palestinian Agricultural Terraces. *Palestine Exploration Quarterly* 107: 65–74.
Gottwald, N. K.
  1974   Were the Early Israelites Pastoral Nomads? Pp. 223–55 in *Rhetorical Criticism: Essays in Honor of James Muilenburg*, eds. J. Jackson and M. Kessler. Pittsburgh: Pickwick.
  1975   Domain Assumptions and Societal Models in the Study of Premonarchic Israel. Pp. 89–100 in *Supplements to Vetus Testamentum* 28 (Edinburgh Congress Volume) ed. G. W. Anderson, et al., Leiden: Brill.
  1976   Israel, Social and Economic Development of. Pp. 465–68 in *Interpreter's Dictionary of the Bible, Supplement Volume*, ed. K. Crim. Nashville: Abingdon.
  1978   The Hypothesis of the Revolutionary Origins of Ancient Israel: a Response to A. J. Hauser and T. L. Thompson. *Journal for the Study of the Old Testament* 7: 37–52.
  1979   *The Tribes of Yahweh: A Sociology of the Religion of Liberated Israel, 1250–1000 B.C.* Maryknoll: Orbis Books.
Harris, M.
  1968   *The Rise of Anthropological Theory: A History of Theories of Culture.* New York: Thomas Y. Crowell.
Heltzer, M.
  1969   Problems of the Social History of Syria in the Late Bronze Age. Pp. 31–46 in vol. 9 of *La Siria nel Tardo Bronzo*, ed. M. Liverani. Rome: Orientis Antiqui Collectio.
Hindess, B., and Hirst, P. Q.
  1975   *Pre-capitalist Modes of Production.* London: Routledge & Kegan Paul.
Jacobsen, T.
  1943   Primitive Democracy in Ancient Mesopotamia. *Journal of Near Eastern Studies* 2: 159–72.
  1957   Early Political Developments in Mesopotamia. *Zeitschrift für Assyriologie* 52: 91–140.
Jankowska, N. B.
  1969   Extended Family Commune and Civil Self-government in Arrapha in the Fifteenth-

Fourteenth Centuries B.C. Pp. 235–52 in *Ancient Mesopotamia: Socio-economic History*, ed. I. M. Diakonoff. Moscow: Nauka.

Klengel, H.
1965–   *Geschichte Syriens im 2. Jahrtausend*, 3 vols. Veröffentlichungen deutsche.
1969
1970   Akademie der wissenschaften zu Berlin Institut für Orientforschung: Akademie-
          Verlag.
1969   Probleme einer politischen Geschichte des spaetbronzezeitlichen Syrien. Pp. 15–
          30 in vol. 9 of *La Siria nel Tardo Bronzo*, ed. M. Liverani. Rome: Orientis
          Antiqui Collectio.

Kosambi, D.
1965   *An Introduction to the Study of Indian History*. Bombay: Popular Book Depot.

Mandel, E.
1971   The Asiatic Mode of Production and the Historical Pre-Conditions for the Rise
          of Capital. Pp. 116–39 in *The Formation of the Economic Thought of Karl Marx*,
          trans. B. Pearce. New York/London: Monthly Review.

Marx, K.
1951   *Marx on China 1853–1860: Articles from the New York Daily Tribune*, introduc-
          tion and notes D. Torr. London: Lawrence & Wishart.
1970   *A Contribution to the Critique of Political Economy*, trans. S. W. Ryazanskaya,
          ed. with introduction M. Dobb. New York: International Publishers.
1973   *Grundrisse. Foundations of the Critique of Political Economy (Rough Draft)*,
          trans. with foreword M. Nicolaus. Baltimore: Penguin.

Mendelsohn, I.
1941   The Canaanite Term for "Free Proletarian." *Bulletin of the American Schools of
          Oriental Research* 83: 36–39.
1955   New Light on the Ḥupšu. *Bulletin of the American Schools of Oriental Research*
          139: 9–11.

Mendenhall, G. E.
1962   The Hebrew Conquest of Palestine. *Biblical Archeologist* 25: 66–87. (Reprinted in
          Biblical Archeologist Reader 3, New York: Doubleday, 1970, pp. 100–20.)
1973   *The Tenth Generation: The Origins of the Biblical Tradition*. Baltimore: Johns
          Hopkins.

Prawar, J., and Eisenstadt, S. N.
1969   Feudalism. *International Encyclopedia of the Social Sciences* 3: 393–403.

Reviv, H.
1972   Some Comments on the Maryannu. *Israel Exploration Journal* 22: 218–28.

Rodinson, M.
1966   *Islam et capitalisme*. Paris: Éditions du Seuil.

Sanders, W., and Price, B.
1968   *Mesoamerica: The Evolution of a Civilization*. New York: Random House.

Wilkinson, J.
1974   Ancient Jerusalem: Its Water Supply and Population. *Palestine Exploration
          Quarterly* 106: 33–51.

Wittfogel, K.
1931   *Wirtschaft und Gesellschaft Chinas. I: Produktivkraefte, Produktions- und Zirkula-
          tionsprozess*. Leipzig: C. L. Hirschfeld.

Wolf, E. R.
1966   *Peasants*. Englewood Cliffs: Prentice-Hall.

Ancient Palestinian Peasant Movements and the Formation of Premonarchic Israel*

MARVIN L. CHANEY

INTRODUCTION

Few biblical scholars would deny that ancient Israel, prior to its coalescence as a monarchic state at the transition from the second to the first millennium B.C., constituted for some time a recognizable society, resident in the hill country of Palestine. An equally broad consensus would probably agree that this premonarchic period proved normative for much in later Israel, but that its detailed, sequential history cannot be written from the information currently available. Although questions concerning the process by which Israel became established in the Palestinian uplands are too important to ignore, the data, of themselves, compel no particular historical reconstruction. As a result, three contending gestalts are presently championed for the historical interpretation of these data.

No full rehearsal of the data is possible or intended here. This study will instead examine the adequacy of the paradigmatic—and frequently controlling—assumptions made by the proponents of each of the three models, while advocating a nuanced version of one. Since these assumptions frequently pertain to societal processes more fully attested in the history of other agrarian societies, a further modicum of control will be sought in the disciplined comparison of such societies by historical sociologists.

*This paper was written while the author was a Visiting Scholar in the Department of Sociology of the University of North Carolina at Chapel Hill, on a sabbatical leave supported by the Association of Theological Schools in the United States and Canada, the Andrew W. Mellon Foundation, the Arthur Vining Davis Foundation, and his home institution, San Francisco Theological Seminary. He gratefully acknowledges the hospitality and support of these institutions. In addition, he wishes to thank Professors C. Calhoun, R. B. Coote, F. M. Cross, N. K. Gottwald, H. A. Landsberger, G. Lenski, W. L. Moran, J. M. Sasson, Mr. T. Sayer, and his wife, R. M. Chaney, from whose critical reading the entire manuscript benefited materially. All errors, whether inadvertent or obstinately maintained in the face of learned critique, remain the sole responsibility of the writer.

The latter expedient is not a methodological commonplace in bibilical studies, and hence deserves a word of explanation. To readers more familiar with the linguistic tools correctly regarded as indispensable to biblical research, the role granted here to the social sciences can be expressed by the following proportion: philology: comparative linguistics::history:historical sociology. The first and third of these fields are primarily concerned with the humanistic interpretation of delimited data— in this case, a given text or a given historical period and location. Utilizing a broader data base, the second and fourth disciplines seek to analyze commonalities of structure, process, and causation. While a tendency to find patterns and make generalizations is thus inherent in the tasks of the two comparative fields, their more delimited counterparts partake of an equal and opposite proclivity for particularism. Only when the tension intrinsic to this division of labor occasions mutually corrective dialogue, rather than polarization, can any of the four disciplines remain healthy.

For example, a difficult form or vocable in the text of the Hebrew Bible routinely prompts a controlled comparison with related phenomena in the other Semitic languages, even though their attestation may be at a great chronological and/or geographical remove. Any study of comparative Semitics is, in turn, dependent upon the fullest possible philological description of Biblical Hebrew. Similarly, when a given event or process in ancient Israelite society is difficult to interpret historically because of sparse or ambiguous data, recourse is properly had to a disciplined comparison of related phenomena in other agrarian societies, just as the comparative analysis of such societies should take account of the most nuanced histories of ancient Israel.

The time is particularly propitious for this dialogue. After a long period of neglect by both anthropology and sociology, agrarian societies— those whose primary means of subsistence is a cultivation of fields which utilizes the plow but not industrial technology—are once again receiving serious attention from social scientists, who, from their side, are expressing renewed interest in interdisciplinary cooperation with historians in the investigation of such societies (Lenski and Lenski 1978: 30, 88–141, 177–230).

Before each of the three models is reviewed in light of this broader methodology, points of congruence among their respective reconstructions need to be sketched, for they are presupposed in the discussion of disputed areas. All would agree that Late Bronze Canaan comprised a miscellany of agrarian city-states, each with its own petty kinglet, but under the nominal suzerainty of Egypt. The power and control of the local dynasts were centered in walled cities which clustered near the steady water supplies of the piedmont springline and the rich, alluvial soils of the plains. Connecting these concentrations of population with each other and the world beyond were overland routes, also favored by the relatively level topography. While constituting only a small minority of the population, the ruling elite were able to dominate the other inhabitants of these plains because they alone could field chariots armed with composite bows. Conversely, premonarchic Israel's poor and mostly unwalled towns and villages were concentrated where the control of the Canaanite kings had never been strong—in the rugged terrain and scrub woods of the hill country. Although this territory was less desirable economically because of its steep, brushy hillsides, thin soils, and relative lack of perennial water sources, it effectively neutralized the tactical advantage of the chariots and composite bows with which the ruling classes held sway on the plains.

With these elements of consensus[1] as background, the conflicting models may be examined.

A MODEL OF NOMADIC INFILTRATION

Developed by such scholars as Alt (1966: 135–69), Noth (1960: 66–84), and, more recently, Weippert (1971: 1–146), what may be termed the no-madic infiltration model posits that the Israelites, prior to their founding of a monarchic state, were land-hungry nomads and semi-nomads in a process of gradual sedentarization in the sparsely inhabited hill country.

> We may think of it as having proceeded rather in the way in which even today semi-nomadic breeders of small cattle from the adjoining steppes and deserts pass over into a settled way of life in the cultivated countryside. . . . The Israelites were land-hungry semi-nomads of that kind before their occupation of the land: they probably first set foot on the land in the process of changing pastures, and in the end they began to settle for good in the sparsely populated parts of the country and then extended their territory from their original domains as occasion offered, the whole process being carried through, to begin with, by peaceful means and without the use of force (Noth 1960: 69).

[1]One partial exception to this consensus is the work of de Geus (1976: 153 and n. 126), who seems to posit the priority and greater density of highland settlement and thereby to explain that "the ancient towns of the Canaanites usually lie on the edge of the plain, at the foot of the mountains" (153). He quotes the work of Baly (1963: 60–78) in support. However, Baly affirms the consensus position and states the real reasons for the location of the cities of Bronze Age Canaan, as follows:

> Almost all the towns mentioned [in Judges 1 as untaken by Israel], it should be noticed, lie in the piedmont region between the still thickly forested uplands and the often marshy districts of the lower-lying plains, for here, where water is most easily available along the piedmont springline, and where movement is less hindered by the nature of the terrain, the greatest settlement had taken place. The only alternative, as Joshua is represented as making clear to the people of Manasseh and Ephraim (Josh 17:18), was to wrestle with the only partly inhabited plateau (62).

The integration of such geographic and demographic factors with those of social stratification and military technology and tactics has been undertaken both historically and sociologically (Yadin 1963: 1–31, 77–356; Rowton 1965: 375–87; Lenski 1966: 189–296; Sjoberg 1960: 80–144 *et passim*).

The latter point is linked by this school with a judgment that Joshua 1–12 is constituted mostly of traditions which were aetiologically generated and hence of little value to the modern historian regarding the events of which they purport to tell (Alt 1936: 13–29; Noth 1953: 7–13; 20–69; Weippert 1971: 136–44). Archaeological evidence for the destruction of many of the cities named in Joshua 10–11 is denied relevance by the judgment that the time and agent(s) of the destruction cannot be ascertained accurately. With military conflict thus largely excluded, the tension between Canaanites and Israelites is understood essentially as that between farmers and nomads, respectively.

Although both past and present exponents of this view exhibit prodigious learning and exert broad influence, their synthesis and its assumptions now stand under heavy and—it would appear to this writer—decisive criticism. The essentials of that critique may be summarized in the following points:[2]

(1) Neither the tribalism of early Israelite society nor the itineracy of some of its members *necessitates* desert or pastoral origins. Tribal organization is well documented among various tillers of the soil, while tinkers, merchants, bandits, and caravaneers itinerate without being desert pastoralists.

(2) In a sharp break with 19th century concepts which still dominate OT scholarship, modern prehistorians and anthropologists no longer regard pastoral nomadism as an evolutionary interval between hunting and gathering and plant cultivation. Instead, it is viewed as a marginal specialization from the animal husbandry which came to be associated with horticulture and agriculture. Thus, although some pastoral nomads might later sedentarize, the evolutionary flow was from the cultivated areas of the Near East "*toward* the steppe and desert, not out of the desert to the sown" (Luke 1965: 24).

(3) So-called "full nomadism," such as that associated with the Midianites or the modern Bedouin, depends upon extensive, mounted use of

---

[2]Mendenhall joined several of these issues, albeit in abbreviated form (1962: 66–87; 1973: 174–97; 1976a: 152–57; 1976b: 132–51). More extensive documentation for much of the summary offered here may be found in several articles by Gottwald (1974: 223–55; 1975: 89–100; 1976b: 629–31; 1978b: 2–7) and the literature which they cite. Access to relevant works by Rowton—in addition to those cited by Gottwald—may be gained through Rowton's recent paper (1977: 181–98). Note should also be taken of the recent work of de Geus (1976: 124–33) and Dever (1977: 102–20).

Weippert's attempt (1971: 102–26) to answer Mendenhall's critique of his understanding of nomadism is largely a précis of the earlier monograph by Kupper (1957). Perhaps most significantly, Weippert (1971: 111, n. 37) indicates awareness of the work of Luke (1965), but states that he has been unable to consult it. Could he have done so, his reply might have been different in kind, for Luke programmatically challenges the assumptions, methods, and conclusions of Kupper. With regard to the Shosu recently discussed by Weippert (1974: 265–80, 427–33), the reader is referred to Gottwald's discussion (1974: 248–51).

camels or horses, which alone allow significant penetration of the Syro-Arabian desert by a preindustrial society. Before the camel saddle made possible the first such penetration, the asses and flocks of "semi-nomads" clung of necessity to the fringes of the fertile crescent. Modern proponents of the nomadic infiltration model recognize that "full nomadism" appeared too late in antiquity to bear upon the discussion of Israelite origins, but their frequent appeal to such intentionally vague phrases as "nomads and semi-nomads" or "(semi-) nomads" endeavors to salvage a paradigm based upon the priority of a nomadism completely at home in the desert. This attempt to win a reprieve for long-cherished assumptions, however, only succeeds in confounding chronological periods, evolutionary sequences, and discrete ecosystems which can and should be distinguished.

(4) Contrary to the dichotomy usually drawn between nomad and farmer, the relationship between cereal cultivation and pastoralism, particularly in its "semi-nomadic" form, was symbiotic. Grain harvest in spring and early summer coincided with the drying up of winter pastures in the steppes. When wetter uplands such as Carmel also proved insufficient, the hungry flocks needed to graze upon the stubble of the harvested grainfields and drink from the perennial waters available where hill met plain. In return, they served as roving manure spreaders, fertilizing the fields for the autumn sowing. At the very least, then, herder and cultivator lived hard by one another several months of each year and were economically inter-dependent; at most, they were one and the same.

(5) Judging from technological parameters and evidence from later periods, the number of pastoral nomads in comparison to the sedentary population would have been quite small. Before the development of a satisfactory camel saddle—which occurred *after* the initial formation of Israel—the number of pastoralists lacking significant intercourse with cultivators may be regarded as historically negligible. The romantic image of the Syro-Arabian desert as a vast womb, producing wave upon wave of Proto-Semites, is as demographically fallacious as it is long-lived in historiography.

(6) Similarly, the portrait of pastoral nomads as the major agents of change in every agrarian society of the ancient Near East has been grossly overdrawn. "Their restiveness and conflict with the state was not due to their invading or infiltrating from the desert but rather to their rural-based resistance to the drafting and taxing powers of the state" (Gottwald 1976b: 629).

(7) OT traditions view the desert as strange and hostile—a place where Israel required special assistance. The motif of "return to desert" has been shown to express a threat against covenant breakers rather than harking back to an idealized past. Other supposed vestiges of a nomadic ideal in the Hebrew Bible, such as the Rechabites, have been plausibly explained in other terms (Riemann 1963: *passim*; Talmon 1966: 31–63; Frick 1971: 279–87).

(8) The land hunger evinced in so many OT texts is far more character-istic of peasants than pastoral nomads (Wolf 1966: *passim*).

(9) The primacy of the aetiological element in Joshua 1–12 posited by Alt and Noth has been convincingly challenged on literary grounds (Seeligmann 1961: 141–69; Childs 1963: 279–92; 1974: 387–97; Long 1968: *passim*).

(10) Modern archaeology has successfully established at more than one site a poor but distinct stratum between the late 13th century destruc-tion of the Late Bronze "Canaanite" city and the appearance of quantities of pottery characteristic of the Philistines. Such strata evidence some building in the ashes of the previous stratum and a material culture consistent with that of the poor, unwalled towns in the hill country which were founded in the same period or refounded then after a long hiatus in occupation. Thus, the likelihood of "Israelites" rather than Philistines or the kings of other Canaanite city-states being the agents of destruction is enhanced (Lapp 1967: 286–87, 292, 298).[3]

Because they stand under this combination of strictures, the axiomatic presuppositions of the nomadic infiltration model fail to inspire confidence.

A CONQUEST MODEL

A second interpretive framework has been forged in polemical dialogue with the nomadic infiltration model. Proponents of this conquest model,[4] as we shall call it, take umbrage, not at the positing of nomadic origins for Israel, but at the treatment of the conquest narratives in Joshua by their opponents. Archaeology has vindicated the essential historicity of these narratives, they argue, by demonstrating that numerous cities stated in the text to have been destroyed do in fact evidence massive destruction:

> . . . the stratigraphic evidence . . . outside the coastal cities and the Plain of Jezreel, points . . . strongly to the thoroughgoing destruction of nearly all important cities in the last half of the 13th century (Lapp 1967: 295).

While Jericho, Ai, and Gibeon are candidly acknowledged as problems because they provide no evidence of occupation at the time,[5] the concatena-tion of destruction layers

---

[3]Mendenhall (1976a: 152–57) now appears to find the agency of the destruction outside Israel. He fails to account adequately, however, for the fact that the cities of the old Canaanite heartland were not destroyed at this time. Only sites located in or near the hill country or otherwise isolated from the main cluster of fortified Canaanite settlements witness destruction late in the 13th century. To state that "such destruction levels are virtually universal at this time throughout the whole of the eastern Mediterranean area" (Mendenhall 1973: 22) glosses over important geographical distinctions.

[4]Prominent here would be the names of Albright, Wright, Bright (especially in the first edition of the work cited below), and Lapp. Most of the relevant bibliography has been collected by Bright (1972: 127, n. 54). Reference may also be made to works of Lapp (1969a: 107–11) and Dever (1974: 44–46) not listed there.

[5]Arad and the Negev, too, raise their own set of problems (Aharoni 1976: 55–76).

. . . certainly suggests that a planned campaign such as that depicted in Josh. 10–11 was carried out. Its purpose was evidently the destruction of the power of the city-states, though some of these states were carefully avoided, presumably because they were too strong. We may safely conclude that during the 13th century a portion at least of the later nation of Israel gained entrance to Palestine by a carefully planned invasion, the purpose of which was not primarily loot but land (Wright 1962: 84).

These destructions and the "poor unfortified occupations that follow, plus the large number of sites with new occupation or with occupation that followed centuries of abandonment," moreover, are thought to "point to a large group of intruders" (Lapp 1967: 295, 299). For the source and nature of these intruders, appeal is had once again to the denizens of the desert or its fringes:

Thus we must conceive of the movement of Hebrew tribes from their nomadic existence into the settled area of urban and agrarian activity, as a movement of uncultured "barbarians" into scenes of self-conscious civilization (Wright 1962: 70).

Although the two mutually antagonistic reconstructions thus share a supposition of Israel's nomadic derivation, the conquest model not only views the intruding Israelites as far more militant, but as more politically self-conscious as well. At the outset of his attempt to give the archaeological evidence historical interpretation, Lapp makes the primacy of political categories a matter of explicit, historiographic theory:

Two observations appear in order in regard to *historical* meaning. First, historical meaning includes political, economic, and cultural aspects. The above evidence has been confined primarily to evidence relating to the political sphere. Cultural objects have been ignored, although the possibility of their shedding light on the political situation has not been overlooked. The second observation is that the bearers of history are not simply people but historical groups, such as Israelites, Philistines, and Canaanites. This observation justifies the focus here on the political sphere. Until the various stratified deposits of archaeological evidence can be confidently attributed to a particular historical group, that evidence can have little specific implication for interpreting economic and cultural history (Lapp 1967: 296).

According to Lapp, then, conflict between Canaanites and Israelites should be understood primarily in political terms.

Even though this writer does not join those who denigrate the archaeological evidence amassed by adherents of the conquest model,[6] he still finds their larger interpretive scheme unconvincing for the following reasons:

(1) Its presumption of the prior existence of "a large group of intruders" as nomads and semi-nomads in the desert suffers all the liabilities already catalogued for such a view.

---

[6]While most earlier excavations and some recent ones have lacked sufficient methodological control, the judgments of Weippert (1971: 127–36) and de Geus (1976: 48–53 *et passim*), following the earlier lead of Noth (1960: 42, 46–48), appear far too sweeping and extreme.

(2) While insisting that the material culture of Israel's earliest settle-ments must be intrusive, proponents have been totally unable to find its antecedents outside Palestine in a manner parallel to that possible, for in-stance, with the Philistines. On the other hand, they are forced to admit that within Palestine, "the basic general typology is virtually identical in the 13th and 12th centuries B.C. (Lapp 1967: 295)." Beyond the specifics of this particular case, an issue of theoretical importance is at stake. Syro-Palestinian archaeologists have tended to explain changes in material culture by the intrusion of new peoples from outside. This tendency is understandable, since much of the hard-won stratigraphy of historical times is fixed by destructions which are attributable to foreign invasions known from literary sources. The broader perspective of important modern theories of sociocultural evolution, however, regards technological innova-tion as a far more frequent and powerful engine of social change than the intrusion of whole new populations.[7] When the external source of a change in material culture is no more apparent than the ubiquitous but highly questionable "(semi-)nomads" of the archaeological literature, the cause of that change is better sought in innovations or conflicts within the society itself or common to all societies in the area.

(3) In their linkage with archaeological evidence, the biblical narra-tives of conquest have been treated selectively. Archaeology has remained necessarily mute on most of the text and openly embarrassing with regard to Jericho, Ai, Gibeon, and Arad, leaving only parts of Joshua 10–11 and Judges 1—the latter exhibiting decidedly gradualist proclivities—to be con-nected with the evidence of material remains.

(4) Treatment of the remaining narratives has tended to be general and unidimensional, as illustrated by the following statement from Lapp:

> . . . the "conquest" by a sizable group is reflected in the Biblical record. It is hard to see how this tradition could have been invented in later times, which could be expected to expand traditions related to the founding of the kingdom by David but hardly to have invented a conquest narrative. This Biblical picture may be stressed without pressing any of its details. The literary stratification is diverse, but it is consistent in indicating a substantial conquest in a rather short period of time (Lapp 1967: 299).

Far from the consistent viewpoint attributed to the text by Lapp, however, the picture of a rapid onslaught from outside, in which all the inhabitants of captured cities were put to the sword, is conveyed primarily if not exclusively by the "Deuteronomistic" framework into which the older

---

[7]Gottwald (1975: 89–100) makes both this point and the fifth one in the discussion that follows. Important theoretical statements of the primacy of technological innovation in social change, couched in probabilistic rather than deterministic terms, have been made by Lenski (1976: 548–64), Lenski and Lenski (1978: 65–85), and Harris (1968: *passim*). Note, too, the role attributed to technology by Sjoberg (1960: 7–13 *et passim*).

literary materials have been set (cf. Miller 1977: 220–21).[8] Moreover, if the "first edition" of the "Deuteronomistic History" is viewed as a programmatic piece written to support the Josianic reform (Cross 1973: 274–89; Freedman 1976: 226–28), its framer's propensities are readily understandable. For that archaizing reform of the late 7th century B.C. sought to weld Judah and the remnants of the northern Kingdom into a united, centralized, pure, and militantly independent nation, realizing its manifest destiny under both Mosaic and Davidic covenants. This program could hardly have been better legitimated than by an interpretation of pre-Davidic history which emphasized the unfailing success of Israel's national and territorial aspirations if and when political cohesion and military discipline were maintained and all vestiges and bearers of "foreign culture" eradicated. Faced with northern suspicions of the centralized leadership of a Davidide, the "Deuteronomistic Historian" urged that the paradigm for such national leadership and its success predated the Davidic monarchy in the person of a northerner—Joshua, the Ephraimite.

(5) Proponents of the conquest model have been inconsistent and imprecise in conceptualizing Canaan, Israel, and their mutual antagonism. On the one hand, Canaan is understood to comprise various agrarian city-states with ever-shifting alliances and enmities, while Israel is envisaged as nomadic tribes, invading from the desert. At a more tacit level, however, following the lead of the "Deuteronomistic Historian," the language used to speak of both seems to presuppose the nation-state as prototype. Lapp's "historical group," a "political" entity to which stratified deposits must be attributed before they can have any "specific implication for interpreting economic and cultural history," appears to be the nation-state in disguise. Wright's "carefully planned invasion" by "a portion at least of the later *nation* [italics mine] of Israel" is cut from the same cloth. But if Canaan was a collection of jealous *city*-states, each with its own petty king, the *nation*-state mold fits premonarchic Israel even less well. Prior to its 13th century occupation of the hill country, it had no territorial definition; prior to David, its poor, unfortified towns and villages witness neither centralized political control nor the extraction and redistribution of a significant economic surplus. In short, the tenuous unity of premonarchic Israel, its lack of sharp social stratification, and its enmity for the city-states of Canaan cannot be explained by the tacit assumption of Israel's prior existence as a nation-state in the desert.[9] The "Deuteronomistic Historian"

[8] The "Deuteronomistic" framework and glosses can be isolated on literary grounds with considerable consistency. Note, for example, the substantial agreement between Noth (1953: 9–10 *et passim*) and Bright (1953: 543 *et passim*) in the delineation of this material, despite the sharp disagreement about the nature of the *pre*-Deuteronomistic text.

[9] The attempt of de Geus (1976: 156–64) to describe early Israel's unity as "primarily ethnic" does not give an adequate causal explanation for the anomalies of Israelite society nor for its hostility toward the kings of Canaan. See n. 1, above, for a critique of de Geus's notion that Bronze Age Canaan witnessed a denser population in the hill country than in the plains.

and many moderns notwithstanding, the nation-state is not always the primary category of history.

As with the nomadic infiltration model, an examination of the conquest model has uncovered many implicit assumptions. Once again, however, these paradigmatic assumptions do not appear viable in the form enunciated.

A MODEL OF PEASANT AND FRONTIER REVOLT

Mendenhall's Hypothesis

Many of the shortcomings of both previous models were first exposed by Mendenhall in his schematic but landmark essay (1962: 66–87).[10] He went on to offer a new hypothesis which sought to evade the pitfalls of the other two:

> The fact is, and the present writer would regard it as a fact though not every detail can be "proven," that both the Amarna materials and the biblical events represent the same political process: namely, the withdrawal, not physically and geographically, but politically and subjectively, of large population groups from any obligation to existing political regimes, and therefore, the renunciation of any protection from these sources. In other words, there was no statistically important invasion of Palestine at the beginning of the twelve tribe system of Israel. There was no radical displacement of population, there was no genocide, there was no large scale driving out of population, only of royal administrators (of necessity!). In summary, there was no real conquest of Palestine in the sense that has usually been understood; what happened instead may be termed, from the point of view of the secular historian interested only in socio-political processes, a peasant's revolt against the network of interlocking Canaanite city-states (Mendenhall 1970: 107).

The catalyst for this movement is seen in a numerically small but ideologically potent Exodus group:

> A group of slave-labor captives succeeded in escaping an intolerable situation in Egypt. Without any other community upon which they could rely for protection and support, they established a relationship with a deity, Yahweh, who had no antecedents except in human traditions about ways in which God manifested himself to human beings (Mendenhall 1970: 107–8).

The Sinai covenant then provided these ex-slaves a minimal blueprint for the formation of a new community in Palestine:

---

[10]Mendenhall's later works (1973: ix–31, 122–214; 1976a: 152–57; 1976b: 132–51) elaborate his views somewhat. Gottwald (1974: 223–55; 1975: 89–100; 1976a: 465–68; 1976b: 629–31; 1978b: 2–7) has followed Mendenhall's lead, but with significant distinctions. In his large volume on the *Tribes of Yahweh: A Sociology of the Religion of Liberated Israel, 1250–1000 B.C.* (Maryknoll, NY: Orbis, 1979) a thorough discussion is provided of the issues raised by the three models.

Common loyalty to a single Overlord, and obligation to a common and simple group of norms created the community, a solidarity which was attractive to all persons suffering under the burden of subjection to a monopoly of power which they had no part in creating, and from which they received virtually nothing but tax-collectors. Consequently, entire groups having a clan or "tribal" organization joined the newly-formed community, identified themselves with the oppressed in Egypt, and received deliverance from bondage (Mendenhall 1970: 108).

This deliverance was effected when

. . . the appearance of the small religious community of Israel polarized the existing population all over the land; some joined, while others, primarily the kings and their supporters, fought. . . . The kings were defeated and forced out . . . (Mendenhall 1970: 113–14).

The broad contours of this hypothesis are attractive because they avoid those weaknesses and inconsistencies which plague the competing reconstructions. Mendenhall's positions have been subjected to numerous criticisms, however, some but not all of which would appear merited.

Mendenhall's Hypothesis Amended

To begin with the former, his heavy, almost exclusive emphasis upon religious ideology as the explanation of premonarchic Israel's social mutations has tended to obscure other important factors. Although Mendenhall speaks of some groups which "migrated to the fringe areas from the more populous regions" (Mendenhall 1970: 114), his gestalt appears far more dominated by "the withdrawal, not physically and geographically, but politically and subjectively, of large population groups from any obligation to the existing political regimes" (Mendenhall 1970: 107). The geographic factor in the withdrawal should not be so easily dismissed. As witnessed by both biblical tradition and archaeology, Israel was not able to take and hold the plains until David's time. The rugged, scrub-covered uplands which it occupied prior to Davidic expansion were, in the Late Bronze Age, the traditional haven for marginal elements who had incurred official disfavor or chosen to withdraw from a more regularized niche in the agrarian society of the plains.[11] Even the language of "official" religion at Ugarit reflected this situation. In a mythic text in which Baal Haddu functions in many regards as a city-state king writ large (*CTA* 4.7.35–37),

Baal's enemies take to the woods,
Haddu's foes to the sides of the mountain crag.

---

[11]Rowton (1965: 375–87) has argued persuasively that ᶜapiru bands, including those of the Amarna Age in Palestine, were centered in just such relatively inaccessible terrain and comprised mostly men who had "withdrawn" from the adjacent city-states.

As shown by the excavations and surface explorations summarized above, such terrain in Palestine sustained a striking growth of unwalled "Israelite" villages on widely dispersed hilltops at the beginning of Iron Age I.[12]

Technological factors were probably responsible for rendering this frontier area habitable by a denser population (Gottwald 1975: 95; Aharoni 1967: 219; de Geus 1975: 65–74; Forbes 1972: 229–32, 244–48; Maddin, Muhly, and Wheeler 1977: 122–31). The introduction of even relatively small amounts of iron, after the Hittite monopoly on smelting techniques was broken, greatly facilitated the clearing and cultivation of the hill country.[13] Rock terraces were also instituted to hold the thin soils and precious seasonal rains of the highland ridge.

> These were best suited to vine, olive, and nut cultivation. But the earliest terrace-farmers at Ai and Khirbet Raddana grew cereals. This inefficient use of terraces suggests an attempt by the highlanders (probably "Israelites" during the period of the Judges) to maintain a subsistence cereal agriculture free from the Canaanite and Philistine spheres, where the primary "bread baskets' were located (Stager 1976: 13).

(It might suggest in addition that these terrace-farmers had previously grown cereals in the plains.) Yet another technological innovation used to be credited with the growth of population in the hills.

> Thanks to the rapid spread of the art, then recent, of constructing cisterns and lining them with waterproof lime plaster instead of the previously used limy marl or raw-lime plaster, the Israelites were able to settle in any site where there was rain, whereas their earlier Canaanite precursors had been forced to restrict their occupation in general to sites near springs or perennial streams (Albright 1960: 113).

While it now appears that this technology was not of such recent origin (Lapp 1969b: 33, n. 53; Paul and Dever 1973: 161; de Geus 1976: 153, n. 127), it was at least available to be expanded and combined with the new technologies, their combination, in turn, allowing the highland ridge to sustain a denser population.

Taken as a whole, these data suggest that the settlements of pre-monarchic Israel be seen as occupying an opening *frontier* of the old city-

---

[12]Campbell (1976: 37–45) and Miller (1977: 252–62) also provide recent summaries of the evidence. Even Weippert (1971: 135) acknowledges the remains of these villages as the one "archaeological fact which can, with a great degree of probability, be connected with the settlement of the 'Israelite' tribes," although he finds the source of this population in sedentarizing semi-nomads.

[13]While 1 Sam 13:19–22 is frequently taken to indicate that the Philistines first introduced iron into Palestine, Aharoni (1967: 219) is probably correct that this Philistine attempt to monopolize iron manufacture "proves that the use of iron tools was already in vogue then in Israel." The Philistines clearly wished Israel to have iron agricultural tools, but under Philistine control and for Philistine profit.

states. Such frontiers in agrarian societies have attracted the interest of social theoreticians

> . . . because they provide a unique opportunity for departures from the sociocultural patterns so deeply entrenched in agrarian societies. Those who respond to the challenge of the frontier, to its dangers and its opportunities, are primarily men with little to lose, with little stake in the established order. Thus they are likely to possess a willingness to take great physical risks and a proclivity for independence and innovation. As a result, new ways of life commonly develop in frontier areas, innovations are readily accepted, and older rigidities give way.
>
> One of the most significant changes that occurs is the breakdown of the traditional class system. . . . Having risked their lives to establish themselves in a new territory, frontiersmen are not prepared to hand over their surplus to anyone. Thus, frontier conditions often break down the sharp inequalities and exploitative patterns characteristic of agrarian societies (Lenski and Lenski 1978: 229).

Dimensions of this sort would seem to constitute an important and necessary complement to Mendenhall's more subjective and ideologically based notions of withdrawal.

His focus on religious ideology has also prompted Mendenhall virtually to equate early Israel's rejection of the forms of socio-political power typically exercised by agrarian states with outright repudiation of the use of socio-political power per se, so that "religion" and "politics" are seen as "reciprocals" (Mendenhall 1973: 198–214; 1975a: 169–80). Early biblical texts, such as Judges 5, corroborate Gottwald's more realistic assessment of the situation: "1) Israel challenged one form of power by means of another form of power, and 2) Israel consciously exercised power even as it consciously attributed the source of all power to its deity" (Gottwald 1975: 94).[14] A less dichotomous understanding of religion and political power also allows the formation of the Israelite monarchy to be viewed less moralistically than "The Fall" depicted by Mendenhall.[15] While kingship and its concomitants were undoubtedly a reversion toward forms more typical of agrarian societies, frontier conditions in such societies are *usually* temporary.

> As . . . the land begins to fill up with people, as roads are built and governmental authority is established, there is a waning of the spirit of independence and individualism, opportunities for resistance decline, and the traditional system begins to assert itself (Lenski and Lenski 1978: 229).

Had Israel not forged its own, separate monarchy upon the anvil of the Philistine crisis, the innovations of its frontier society might have been

---

[14] In this regard, note should also be taken of Mendenhall's own reluctant acknowledgement (1973: 137, n. 72) and Holladay's review (1973: 472–74).

[15] In addition to the works of Mendenhall already cited, note his explicit treatment of the monarchy (1975b: 155–70). That his more schematic formulations, including that of the "tenth generation," sometimes involve this same moralizing has been noted by reviewers (Sasson 1974: 294–96).

crushed forever beneath the tyrant's heel. As it was, those innovations—particularly in their prophetic expression—not only bent Israelite monarchy significantly, but also outlived it to exert influences still strongly felt today.

While it would be unfair to press the language of Mendenhall's brief article too hard, such statements as, "the appearance of the small religious community of Israel polarized the existing population all over the land" (Mendenhall 1970: 113), appear to many readers to adhere more closely to ideological predilection than historical reality. Peasant movements typically involve long periods of smoldering unrest with much if not most of the populace neutral, conservatively indifferent, or involved in cleavages and conflicts which crosscut and attenuate a polarization between peasants and ruling elite (Landsberger 1973: 1–64). Early Israel's lack of territorial contiguity, its abundance of natural barriers even within contiguous areas, its inclusion of many microclimates, each with its own variations in the means of subsistence, and its biblical description as a "mixed multitude" all suggest that no polarization of "Israelite" peasantry could be quick, easy, or complete. Since archaeology and biblical traditions also witness great turmoil *internal* to premonarchic Israel, categories designed to investigate these cleavages belong in any framework for the analysis of early Israelite society.

Although each of these attempts to nuance or supplement Mendenhall's model of a peasant revolt involves matters of significance, seen in the broader context, they amount to "praising with faint damns," for they serve to reaffirm the basic cogency and heuristic value of such a model. Other critics have sought to find more fundamental flaws in this paradigm, however, and they deserve reply.

Response to Criticisms of Mendenhall's Treatment of Nomadism and the Amarna Letters

As already noted (n. 2, above), Weippert's attempt to rehabilitate a notion of Israel's nomadic origin in the desert reiterates the older position and its assumptions, without really confronting the mounting critique which renders it untenable.

The critique of Mendenhall's use of the 14th century B.C. diplomatic archive, discovered at El-Amarna on the middle Nile and commonly known as the Amarna letters, must occupy us longer, even though only a summary of the complex issues involved is possible here. Particularly crucial is his interpretation of the social dynamics associated with the term *ᶜapiru/SA.GAZ* as it is employed by the petty kinglets of Syro-Palestine in correspondence with their nominal suzerain, the Pharaoh of Egypt. Since the nature and identity of these *ᶜapiru* and their possible relation to the "Hebrews" (*ᶜibrî*) and "Israelites" of the Hebrew Bible have been the subject of a voluminous and polemical literature,[16] areas of general consensus among Mendenhall, his published critics, and the majority of informed opinion are probably best stated first: (1) The Amarna ʿapiru were autochthonous in Syro-Palestine, rather than constituting an invasion —nomadic or otherwise—from outside (Weippert 1971: 71; de Geus 1976: 184, 186). (2) Despite recent attempts to revive earlier notions, ʿapiru is not primarily or originally an ethnic designation.[17] (3) Instead, it refers basically to various elements in the population who were declassed, fugitive, uprooted, or who otherwise stood outside the acknowledged social system (Weippert 1971: 58, 65; de Geus 1976: 182–83; Rowton 1976a: 13–20; Mendenhall 1973: 122–24). (4) In a semantic generalization probably assisted by the ambiguity of such a negatively defined appellation, ʿapiru was not infrequently broadened in the Amarna correspondence to serve as a pejorative designation of one's enemies, vilifying them to the Egyptian court (Weippert 1971: 72–74; Mendenhall 1973: 123–24, 130–35; Campbell 1960: 13–15). (5) Early discussion of the ʿapiru often focused upon the term's etymology. While there is some continuation of that trend, a growing consensus views the etymological arguments as moot and of little *historical* significance (Weippert 1971: 82–83; de Geus 1976: 184–85; Rowton 1976a: 13–15).[18]

Beyond these areas of broad agreement lie major disputes. Reacting in part to the unnuanced brevity of Mendenhall's initial suggestion that the Amarna ʿapiru were engaged in a "peasant's revolt," Weippert has sought to demonstrate that the movement was "purely political":

The texts clearly state that city kings, princes, countries, 'mayors' (*ḫazannūtu*), cities (communities of citizens), *ḫupšu* belong to the ʿapiru or join with them. . . . The tenor of all the references . . . indicates that the writers of the letters, who remained faithful to the Egyptian crown or at least wished to appear faithful in their letters to the Pharaoh or to high officials, mean by ʿapiru, amongst whom they classify many of their colleagues (mostly their personal enemies), simply rebels against Egyptian sovereignty and are able, at the same time, to give the term an additional pejorative sense (Weippert 1971: 71–72).

Weippert then concludes that

. . . our observation of the fact that local kings and their followers took part in the rebellion, shows us beyond all shadow of a doubt that the ʿapiru revolt in the Amarna

---

[16]Access to this literature may be had through the recent work of Rowton (1976a: 13, n. 2) and de Geus (1976: 182–83, nn. 236–43).

[17]While some scholars have recently reverted to an ethnic understanding of ʿapiru (Astour 1976: 382–85; de Geus 1976: 182, n. 237), the bases for such an interpretation have received decisive critique (Weippert 1971: 70; de Geus 1976: 182–83; Rowton 1976a: 17; Mendenhall 1973: 122–24).

[18]Mendenhall has recently discussed etymology again (1973: 128–41), but his etymology builds upon his historical description, not the reverse.

period was not an uprising on the part of the oppressed population of the plains
against the ruling feudal classes of the cities and is certainly not to be understood on
the basis of a comparison with the great German Peasants' Revolt of 1525/26
(Weippert 1971: 74).

Unlike Weippert, de Geus wrote after the publication of Mendenhall's
essay, "The ʿApiru Movements in the Late Bronze Age" (1973: 122–41), but
his refutation with regard to Amarna is limited to one sentence: "To speak,
with Mendenhall, of social revolt, is going too far (de Geus 1976: 184 and
n. 245)."

While mere expressions of opinion require no answer, Weippert's
objections do. As stated, they are both semantically and sociologically
simplistic because they assume a completely consistent use of the term
ʿapiru in the Amarna archive and an unalloyed homogeneity in their
constituency, motivation, and leadership of the social and political
movements to whose members it was applied. Both assumptions are
intrinsically improbable and demonstrably false with regard to the Amarna
ʿapiru. Weippert himself recognizes that ʿapiru is basically a socio-economic
designation outside Amarna and that its supposed use there to specify
"simply rebels against Egyptian sovereignty" is derived (Weippert 1971: 65–
74). Although one would hardly expect the extension of the term to a
political slur to abandon or erase completely all remnants of its former
meaning, such subjective judgments need not bear the burden of the
argument. For even Weippert (1971: 68, 73) grudgingly admits that ʿapiru
was employed in the Amarna letters explicitly to denote declassed elements
who served as mercenaries *in the Egyptian cause* (*EA* 195: 24–32), as well
as brigands who took advantage of the troubled times (*EA* 318: 8–15).[19] To
these passages should be added *EA* 112: 43–47, not mentioned by Weippert, in which Rib-Adda of Byblos, purportedly the staunchest of all supporters of Egyptian hegemony in Syro-Palestine, rewards an ʿapiru for
serving as his messenger.

Exceptions to Weippert's monolithic understanding of the Amarna
ʿapiru do not stop there. While instances of political opportunism on the
part of groups and leaders called ʿapiru certainly abound in the letters,
their intrigue and hostility are directed only partially and often tangentially
against Egyptian suzerainty. The major targets of ʿapiru activity are the
petty dynasts of the Syro-Palestinian city-states (cf. *EA* 68:12–18; 73:14–
33; 74:19–41; 75:10–11; 76:7–20; 77:21–37; 79:7–29; 81:6–13; 85:63–82;
88:29–34; 90:5–25; 91:3–26; 104:17–54; 117:35–40, 56–64, 92–94; 118:21–39;
130:36–42; 144:22–32; 246 rev.: 5–10; 271:9–21; 272:10–17; 273:8–24;
286:16–60; 287:14–24; 288:36–46; 299:17–26; 305:21–24; 318:8–15; 366:11–
26), who are under fire from elements of what is ostensibly their own

---

[19]For ʿapiru as mercenaries, see also *EA* 71:10–31; 246:5–10. Citation of the Amarna
archive follows the numbering of Knudtzon (1915) and Rainey (1970).

population (basic sense of *ᶜapiru*), from other such dynasts taking advantage of chaotic conditions for self-aggrandizement at their neighbors' expense (derived sense of *ᶜapriu*), or some combination of the two. Although Rib-Adda sought to convince his suzerain that the *ᶜapiru*-linked activities of Abdi-Ashirta and Aziru were blatantly anti-Egyptian, the court policies of "balance of power" and "divide and rule" apparently viewed Rib-Adda's constant appeals as alarmist and self-serving: they were largely ignored as being Rib-Adda's concern, not Pharaoh's (cf., e.g., *EA* 106:13–16). *EA* 101:29–31 and 161:51–53, moreover, speak of the placement of Abdi-Ashirta and Aziru in their positions *by the Egyptian crown* (cf. Mendenhall 1973: 125–27; *EA* 60; and, on *EA* 101, Moran 1969: 94–99). That Aziru later defected to the Hittites does not alter the fact that both he and his father served by Egyptian appointment and regularization of their de facto power while Rib-Adda accused them of being or consorting with *ᶜapiru*. On the other hand, the self-righteously "loyal" Rib-Adda not only threatened to make a pact with Abdi-Ashirta (*EA* 83:23–27), following the pattern of other dynasts in the area (*EA* 82:5–13; 85:63–69), but, it would now appear (McCarter 1973: 15–18), actually attempted such collusion with Aziru. In short, both the term *ᶜapiru* in Amarna usage and the activities to which it was applied are far more complex than simple rebellion against Egyptian sovereignty.

Similarly, Weippert's claim that the Amarna materials cannot reflect popular uprisings because the term *ᶜapiru* is applied to local kinglets and their followers is specious on any of three grounds: (1) Such application of the term is easily explained as political slurring, which proves nothing about the possibility of its use elsewhere in a more specific, socioeconomic sense. (To refer to a modern analogue, the status and attributes of persons to whom the terms "communist" or "fascist" have been hostilely applied could hardly be used to deny any particular trait to social and political movements more specifically designated by these names.) (2) Peasant movements enjoying more than localized and momentary success have always involved and allied with other, non-peasant elements—the more successful, the less "pure" (Landsberger 1973: 1–64, esp. 57–60). (According to Weippert's historiographic principles, the English Peasant Revolt of 1381 could not have involved a peasant revolt because prominent landowners —including Sir Roger Bacon—and three of London's aldermen are known to have been participants and/or allies.) (3) Most important, while the sparse contexts of many of the Amarna occurrences of *ᶜapiru* might permit various understandings of the term, other passages slighted or ignored by Weippert clearly reflect social unrest.[20] Because of the importance and complexity of this material, a representative sample has been translated

---

[20]Nor has this unrest gone unnoticed in the secondary literature (Artzi 1964: 159–66; Astour 1964: 6–17; Moran 1967: 878–80; Liverani 1965: 267–77; 1974: 352–55).

and discussed in an excursus, "The ᶜApiru and Social Unrest in the Amarna Letters from Syro-Palestine" (see below, pp. 72–81).

Even presuming the social agitation documented there in connection with the Amarna ᶜapiru, their exact relation to the "Hebrews" (ᶜibrî) and "Israelites" of the Hebrew Bible remains to be treated. Weippert himself concludes from a full investigation of the relevant phonological and morphological data that "the equation ᶜapiru = Hebrews can certainly be substantiated with linguistic proofs" (1971: 82, cf. 74–82, 101). He then surveys by category the thirty-three biblical occurrences of ᶜibrî(m), agreeing that the "Hebrew slave" of OT legal texts can be compared with the ᶜapiru in slavery contracts from Nuzi, and allowing some analogy between the Amarna ᶜapiru and the use of "Hebrew" in 1 Samuel to designate both Israelites who serve the Philistines as mercenaries and the opposing Israelite forces themselves (Weippert 1971: 101, cf. 85–88). Otherwise, he regards all connections with grave suspicion:

> The passages in the Joseph story and the exodus narratives, as well as the examples from late Old Testament and subsequent writings, seem to understand the word ᶜibrî as an archaic way of describing the 'Israelite' nation. The connection with the ᶜapiru is extremely indirect (Weippert 1971: 101).

From this fact and the occurrence of ᶜibrî(m) only in certain circumscribed groups of texts, Weippert concludes that it "seems out of the question to regard without closer examination the terms 'Hebrews' and 'Israelites' as synonyms and to lump the 'Israelites'/'Hebrews' together with the ᶜapiru-people" (1971: 101).

Although the brevity of Mendenhall's initial article might be read as failing to make such distinctions adequately, recent discussions provide nuanced answers to Weippert's objections (Mendenhall 1973: 135–38; Rowton 1976a: 19). Rowton (1976a: 19) cites both old and new evidence for the employment of ᶜapiru labor on Egyptian building operations, paralleling the use of ᶜibrî(m) in several of the Exodus narratives. Regarding the alternation of "(Yahweh), God of the ᶜibrîm" with "Yahweh, God of Israel" in these narratives, he writes:

> these detribalized Israelites who, to an Egyptian or or [sic] a Philistine, amounted to little more than tribal scum and renegades, would have been viewed in Israelite tradition as tribal expatriates. Hence from this view, "God of the ᶜibrîm" is simply equivalent to "God of the tribal expatriates," meaning, of course, in the context in which it occurs, Israel's expatriates. And could it be seriously suggested that Jahwe would not have been credited with the power to protect an Israelite living among foreigners? (Rowton 1976a: 20).

In these Exodus passages and those where Weippert admits some relationship with ᶜapiru, the term ᶜibrî(m) would appear to reflect its socio-economic and *Politico*-legal roots. All these "Hebrews" were ᶜapiru, in that sense, though, of course, not all ᶜapiru were "Hebrews," the former term finding a much wider expression geographically and chronologically. When the monarchic state of Israel coalesced about David and his "Hebrew" band, however, this formerly social designation could gradually have acquired an "ethnic" connotation. Rowton offers cogent parallels for such a development, and terms the resulting appellation a "social ethnonym" (1976a: 9–20, esp. 19; cf. Mendenhall 1973: 137). Since virtually all texts in the Hebrew Bible which employ *ᶜibrî(m)* were written after the advent of the monarchy, it should occasion no surprise that many of them evidence ambiguity between social and "ethnic" meanings for the term, with some knowing only the latter.

Several conclusions seem clear: (1) There is no definitive bar to connecting *ᶜapiru* and *ᶜibrî(m)* linguistically. (2) Quite apart from any etymological link, many of the *ᶜibrî(m)* of the Hebrew Bible occupy social roles analogous to the *ᶜapiru* of cuneiform and Egyptian sources. (3) Other occurrences of *ᶜibrî(m)* appear to witness the term's development into a "social ethnonym," a process well documented elsewhere and readily intelligible within the historical context. Development in the opposite dirction is implausible. (4) Because of this development, OT texts taken as a whole are ambiguous about the relationship between "Hebrews" and "Israelites." From the perspective of *monarchic* "Israel," *all* Israelites, particularly those in foreign contexts, could be called "Hebrews" as an archaic, "ethnic" name, or some Israelites could be called "Hebrews" to designate their social role. As seen above, however, *most* members of the *pre*monarchic federation known as "Israel" were "Hebrews" in the socioeconomic and *politico - legal* sense. (5) All names and their possible linguistic associations aside, premonarchic Israel held in common with the Amarna *ᶜapiru* of an earlier time their geographic, social, and tactical location, significant forms of social organization, and the enmity of the kinglets of the same Canaanite city-states. (6) Since major interventions in the Palestinian hill country by Egypt or other monarchic states are unknown between the Amarna Age and the appearance of premonarchic Israel, considerable continuity of social dynamic is probable. (7) In the historical reconstruction of premonarchic Israel, therefore, reference to the social unrest unequivocally attested for Syro-Palestine by the Amarna archive is legitimate on *historical* grounds, and does not rest upon a semantically simple-minded equation of *ᶜapiru*, "Hebrews," and "Israelites." All three terms entail decided ambiguity, and their referents vary with the context; no two are completely synonymous; each is closely related to the others in the manner outlined.

Archaeological Objections to the Revolt Model Considered

Even when Mendenhall is granted use of the Amarna materials, however, his hypothesis still faces criticism from proponents of the conquest model, who have argued that archaeological evidence weighs against notions of a peasant revolt. Lapp is most explicit:

> But the massive destructions and the complete reorientations of fairly prosperous cities
> could hardly have resulted so consistently, I would expect, if the primary matter was
> the elimination of a few Canaanite overlords. The employment of so many silos (not
> known in the Late Bronze age), the new kind of ceramic ware, the architectural
> poverty, and the new occupations on so many sites combine to suggest a social change
> that is more than the result of social upheaval. These things point to a large group of
> intruders. The "revolt of the masses" seems to be a modern construct forced on ancient
> traditions in opposition to the archaeological evidence (1967: 298–99).

As we have already seen (n. 3, above), Mendenhall's current answer seems
to be that the agent of destruction was not Israel. He has recourse instead
to what he terms the virtual universality of destruction levels at this time in
the whole eastern Mediterranean area.

Painting with that broad a brush glosses over important distinctions
which may be briefly summarized: (1) In the late 13th and early 12th
centuries B.C., the destruction in Palestine took place at sites in or near
the hill country or otherwise isolated from the main group of Canaanite city-states, which were *not* destroyed at that time. (2) Away from
the coast, more than one site evidences the sequence: Late Bronze
Canaanite, "Israelite" (material culture consistent with the unwalled villages
of the hill country), and Philistine. Some such "Israelite" towns were built
in the ashes of the previous Canaanite city (Lapp 1967: 286–87, 292, 298).
(3) At least some cities in the coastal plain have no "Israelite" stratum in
the period concerned, but passed directly from the destruction of the "Canaanite" city to Philistine occupation (Lapp 1967: 293–94; Miller 1977:
257). (4) In other instances (e.g., Shechem and Khirbet Rabûd), no layer of
destruction separates the "Canaanite" and "Israelite" strata (Campbell
1975: 152–53).

Although these distinctions tend to erode Mendenhall's position on the
archaeological evidence, they aid in formulating an alternative answer to
Lapp's objections which is consistent with Mendenhall's hypothesis as
amended here. This answer may be developed by discussing seriatim the
categories of data which Lapp thinks to necessitate "a large group of
intruders" and tell against a popular uprising.

He looks first to "the massive destructions and complete reorientations
of fairly prosperous cities," phenomena which also trouble E. F. Campbell
(1975: 152), who is considerably less hostile to Mendenhall's approach. But
one must ask what was destroyed, and what, for that matter, has been
excavated. With few exceptions, the answer is the same—the city fortifications and the temple-palace-garrison-store house-elite housing complexes.
These structures were instruments and symbols of the power and social
control of the governing class, requiring corvée labor to build. As in most
agrarian societies, they stood as architectural manifestations of a system of
stratification in which an elite of probably no more than two percent of the
population controlled up to half or more of the total goods and services
produced (Lenski 1966: 189–296; Lenski and Lenski 1978: 177–230; Sjoberg

1960: 80–107, 110, *et passim*).[21] An internal revolt against this small governing class and any of its retainers who remained loyal, therefore, would have involved an attack upon these very structures for reasons both "instrumental" and "expressive."[22] All but the briefest fighting would have resulted in the destruction of some non-elite structures as well, for the forces which ultimately won would probably have sustained reverses in the process, and fire, once unleashed in the preindustrial city, would have been almost impossible to control. In any reoccupation by the "revolutionaries," architectural poverty and reorientation would certainly have been the order of the day, since, at the level of technology then current, to do otherwise would have meant the reimposition of the very exactions and corvée they had bought to abolish. Cities where the governing class fled, or where it chose to conciliate its people and the loose federation known as Israel, would not have experienced such radical architectural disruption, but the marked reduction in social stratification and division of labor would have resulted in material culture similar to that of the people who reoccupied the destroyed cities and founded the many new villages of this period.[23]

Let us now examine that material culture more closely. Lapp argues that the pit silo, whose profusion is the virtual trademark of the earliest "Israelite" sites, was unknown in the Late Bronze Age, and that it was therefore introduced from outside Palestine, even though he cannot point to antecedents elsewhere. Although pit silos may have been as rare in Late Bronze Canaan as they were frequent in early Iron I "Israel," they *did* exist. Albright reports finding several at Tell Beit Mirsim in strata unequivocally belonging to the Late Bronze Age (Albright 1932: 51; 1938: 64–65; 1943: 1–4). Nor is the rapid proliferation in earliest "Israel" of this minor form of "Canaanite" grain storage difficult to explain in terms of a model of peasant and frontier revolt. Because the surrender by the peasants to the ruling class of a large proportion of their cereal harvest would have been a major source of conflict (for the Amarna Age, cf. Albright, 1975: 106), one would expect peasants who had overthrown or driven out their lords to institute a radically decentralized means of storing the grain which they had thereby redeemed from the tax-collector. The pit silo, which is found in

[21]To those who would protest that no such statistical data are available from Late Bronze Canaan, it must be answered that these figures have been developed on a broadly comparative basis for agrarian societies as a type of social and economic organization. The system of stratification described is *generic* to societies based upon a cultivation technology which knows the plow but not the industrial revolution. For all their cultural and historical diversity, therefore, the variations within any such society are far greater than between any two such societies.

[22]Landsberger (1973: 21–22) provides a convenient explanation of these terms and a convincing argument that they properly represent two separate dimensions, which are by no means mutually exclusive.

[23]Campbell (1975: 152–53) makes a similar assessment of the evidence from such sites as Shechem and Khirbet Rabûd.

most, but not all early Israelite towns and villages (Callaway 1976: 29–30) would have represented one cheap and available method for keeping precious cereals hard by the dwelling of the peasant who had produced them.

Similar considerations readily explain the rapid growth in the population of the hill country witnessed by the founding of many new and widely dispersed villages and the reoccupation of other sites long vacant. Retention by the peasants of surpluses formerly surrendered to the ruling elite of the few upland cities would have been partially responsible, for as Mendenhall rightly states, "peasant populations tend to invest economic surpluses in population increase" (Mendenhall 1976a: 157). Another cause of this denser population has already been outlined in terms of the technological innovations which rendered the highland ridge a more economically viable haven for disgruntled peasants from the plains. Callaway provides a specific example. In a discussion of the early "Israelite" village founded upon the long-deserted mound at Ai, he notes the similarity between a terrace-creating retainer wall there and "barriers built in valleys or wadi beds to slow the flow of water and trap eroded soil. . . . Because of the similarity of the terraces and barriers built in valleys, one may conjecture an origin for the villagers in the lowland region west of the hill country" (Callaway 1976: 29–30). Flight to the hill country would have put such villagers beyond the effective control of their former lords, for the terrain itself helped to neutralize the dread chariots with which those lords dominated the plains. Thus free from high taxes and rents on their agricultural production and from the imposition of corvée in order to build city walls and monumental architecture, these newcomers to the hills would also have retained economic surpluses, thereby adding to the process of "swarming" noted by Mendenhall (1976a: 157).

Lapp's final objection concerns pottery, regarding which his own masterful summary (1967: 295–96) marks the following salient features: (1) "The basic general typology is virtually identical in the 13th and 12th centuries B.C." (2) "Both periods are characterized by very heavy vessels, . . ." but ". . . the Late Bronze ware seems to be much more finely levigated, and many of the diverse particles characteristic of Iron I ware do not seem to occur in the Late Bronze ware." (3) Differences in color "suggest different kiln traditions." (4) By the 12th century, both imports and their local imitations cease outside the coastal and Esdraelon plains. Once again, this evidence no more necessitates "a large group of intruders" than it precludes the paradigm developed here. In the highly stratified society of the Canaanite city-states, artisan skills were relatively specialized and foreign trade, consisting principally of luxury and strategic goods, had been developed by and for the ruling elite. One would expect imported pottery under such circumstances, with local, full-time potters throwing well refined clay and utilizing relatively sophisticated and consistent techniques of firing. If premonarchic Israel constituted the kind of frontier counter-formation from this Canaanite society here presumed, it could be expected to employ part-time potters who would carry on the same basic ceramic typology in utilitarian vessels, but with cruder execution. Local clay, often less well refined, would be fired under more rudimentary and less consistent conditions. Since this subsistence economy would not produce major concentrations of wealth or trade in either luxury wares or commodities, imported pottery would not appear. In short, a model of peasant and frontier revolt accounts for this and the other archaeological evidence cited by Lapp at least as well as, if not better than, a large group of conquerors from outside. Since the antecedents and subsistence of any such group outside Palestine are problematic in the extreme, the balance of probability in accounting for the archaeological data falls to a model of revolt and withdrawal toward an opening frontier.

Conditions Conducive to Peasant Revolt

Yet another frequent objection to such a model contends that it "seems to be a modern construct superimposed upon the biblical traditions" (Miller 1977: 279; cf. Lapp 1967: 299), and that it "seems altogether too idealistic and romantic" (de Geus 1976: 186)! But these opinions are merely asserted rather than argued, and ignore both the Amarna evidence cited here and the fact that the history of agrarian societies is replete with peasant rebellions (Lenski 1966: 274–75; Wolf 1969: 279; Landsberger 1973: 1). Particularly pertinent is a burgeoning literature which studies comparatively those far fewer peasant movements which have grown to more than localized extent and significance. While such comparative studies cannot prove that ancient Israel emerged from a Palestinian peasant's revolt, they can allow us to determine whether there existed in Late Bronze and early Iron I Palestine a concatenation of conditions which in other agrarian societies have proved conducive to broader peasant revolts.

What, in summary, are some of those circumstances, as they have been delineated by historically minded scientists? Wolf argues convincingly that the "tactically mobile" segment of a peasantry is the most likely to revolt because such peasants "are able to rely on some external power to challenge the power which constrains them" (1969: 290). Furthermore, "any factor which serves to increase the latitude granted by that tactical mobility reinforces their revolutionary potential" (1969: 293). Although controversy abounds concerning which stratum of the peasantry in areas under close landlord control best meets the revolutionary criteria (Landsberger 1973: 17–18, 26), there is broad agreement that "peripheral location with regard to the center of state control" *does* grant such latitude (Wolf 1969: 293; cf. Lenski 1966: 274). "The tactical effectiveness of such areas is strengthened still further if they contain defensible mountain redoubts" (Wolf 1969: 293). Both the Amarna ᶜapiru and premonarchic Israel, of course, occupied the mountainous periphery of the Canaanite city-states.

More romantic notions notwithstanding, the unequal economic relationship between elite and peasantry has not, of itself, produced peasant
revolutions. Landlords have frequently provided protection and other
services necessary for the agricultural cycle and social cohesion of the
village, thus forming manystranded bonds with their peasants. "Where the
links arising out of this relationship between overlord and peasant community are strong, the tendency toward peasant rebellion (and later revolution) is feeble" (Moore 1966: 469). The failure of the aristocracy to perform
such compensatory services for the peasantry, however, reduces the relationship to a single strand, one of economic exploitation. This turn of affairs is
both obvious to peasants and conducive to revolt (Moore 1966: 468–71;
Landsberger 1973: 29–30). As the Amarna letters (see below, pp. 72–81)
and anepigraphic archaeology both make clear, Palestine, just prior to and
during the emergence of Israel as a society, was embroiled in a chronic
state of petty warfare, with none of the local dynasts able effectively to
protect his peasants or their fields.

These constant hostilities would have had results other than imposing
additional economic burdens on the peasantry and undermining the strength
and effectiveness of the ruling class. "Indeed, wars in general are associated
with, and often precede the outbreak of peasant unrest" (Landsberger 1973:
52). Of particular relevance here is the consciousness-arousing aspect of
peasant involvement in warfare, for "individuals and groups most likely to
participate in peasant organizations are those whose traditional values have
been modified . . . through such circumstances as participation in military
service and war" (Landsberger 1969: 41). As a result of this experience,
"skill in the disciplined use of force is acquired, the fruits of organization
and cooperation [are] observed and often the incompetence of the upper
strata demonstrated" (Landsberger 1973: 52). The descriptions of certain
ḫupšu in the Amarna letters indicate that some Syro-Palestinian peasants
gained such experience and acted accordingly. That the term apparently
means both "peasant" and "peasant soldier" also seems to reflect the
enlistment of numerous peasants into armed service (see below, pp. 73–75),
and n. 31).

Structural considerations are also significant. "The great agrarian bureaucracies of royal absolutism . . . have been especially liable to the combination of factors favoring peasant revolution" (Moore 1966: 478; cf.
472–74; 478–79; and Landsberger 1973: 30). They have tended to take over
the protective and judicial functions of the local overlord, and thus to
weaken the crucial ties between peasants and the upper classes. Where their
assumption of these functions has been only partial and/or when royal
power has waned, two overlapping and competing layers of administration
have usually developed, each exacting an economic surplus from the
peasants, but neither able or willing to protect their persons or production.
Corruption and bribery have run rife under such conditions. Due partially

to environmental factors, Egypt provides the most striking example from the ancient Near East of royal absolutism and its attendant bureaucracy (Parsons 1977: 53–63). When the Pharaohs of the New Kingdom period extended Egyptian rule into Palestine, compromises were struck between the kind of bureaucratic control which was possible in the Nile valley and the exegencies of distance, terrain, and entrenched local overlords—a situation which was repeated a millennium later under Ptolemaic administration (Helck 1962: 109–621; Lorton 1974: 176–79 *et passim*; Albright 1975: 102–16; Tcherikover 1959: 59–73; Bagnall 1976: 11–24). As a result, neither the Egyptian "commissioners" nor the local Canaanite "governors"—*rabiṣūtu* and *ḫazannūtu*, respectively, in Amarna parlance—could effectively maintain order in the absence of an Egyptian army, but both could and did extract resources from the peasants of Canaan. "The extent to which both official and irregular exaction went is almost unbelievable" (Albright 1975: 106).

In addition to this situation of double taxation without compensation, "reinforcing cleavages," such as national, religious, ethnic, and linguistic divisions, have been found to enhance the revolutionary potential of peasants. "Cleavages other than economic ones may be of critical importance both in strengthening and weakening peasant movements, depending simply on whether or not they coincide with, or cut across class lines" (Landsberger 1973: 54; cf. Wolf 1969: 293). One such reinforcing cleavage of an ethnic nature is suggested for Canaan by the fact that "a high proportion of the Palestinian chiefs bore Indo-Aryan names," while "the proportion of Indo-Aryans decreases as we go downward in the social scale" (Albright 1975: 104, 109).

This reinforcement of a stark vertical differentiation was linked with a relative lack of horizontal differentiation in the structure of Canaanite society—that is, economic, political, religious, and other institutions were quite incompletely distinguished. Such a combination favored profound and wide-ranging goals in any peasant movement which might arise, for "the more the social institutions confronting the peasant were themselves interconnected—so that in order to tackle one, they all had to be dealt with—the broader would be the movement's goals" (Landsberger 1973: 25; cf. 1969: 31–35).

The revolutionary tendencies of peasants have also been shown to vary in relation to the institutional structure of the peasant village itself. "In a rebellious and revolutionary form of solidarity, institutional arrangements are such as to spread grievances through the peasant community and turn it into a solidarity group hostile to the overlord" (Moore 1966: 475). Landsberger writes of "a history of communal cooperative effort" favoring a "common reaction to low status" (1973: 27). Recent, detailed studies of the documentary evidence from Syria for village life in the Late Bronze Age have emphasized the collective nature of many obligations.

Villages, as collective units, were obligated to meet all taxes and duties placed upon them by the royal government. This demonstrates the communal character of the Ugaritic village, which should thus be considered a rural community (Heltzer 1976; 47).

The rural communities were collectively responsible for corvée, . . . [and] . . . in various legal actions (Heltzer 1976: 63).

Heltzer (1976: 1, 102) is undoubtedly correct that these conclusions may be extrapolated, *mutatis mutandis*, to Palestine, since the pressures of commercialization, which tend to erode such arrangements, were stronger at Ugarit than in Palestine.

Perhaps the most significant such institutional arrangement was a system of land tenure wherein the fields were held by the village as a whole and were periodically redistributed among its members to take account of demographic changes. "One of the main consequences of the periodic redivision of property in the . . . peasant commune . . . seems to have been to generalize land hunger, to align the richer peasants with the poorer ones" (Moore 1966: 475–76). Although seriously attenuated by elite and mercantile encroachments, some vestiges of this system seem to be reflected in the Syrian evidence (Heltzer 1976: 65–71; Diakonoff 1975: 121–33). Moreover, as virtually all students of the subject have concluded (Alt 1955: 13–23; 1959: 348–72; Bess 1963: *passim*), only the postulation of this repartitional domain for premonarchic Israel and of its unequal conflict with the combination of patrimonial and prebendal domain[24] introduced in conjunction with the monarchy can adequately account for scores of allusions in the Hebrew Bible. The origins of this system and the accompanying generalization of land hunger should not be sought, with Alt and his followers, among sedentarizing nomads, for such an explanation is predicated upon a model the evidentiary bases of which have been almost completely eroded. Since repartitional domain is well attested in the historical record of agrarian socieites,[25] and administrative texts seem to support its prior existence in Syro-Palestine, the roots of this phenomenon in Israel are best traced to the villages of Canaan. The ideology of the Exodus group added the potent notion that all the land ultimately belonged to Yahweh, the only legitimate overlord, thereby stripping of legitimation any absolute claim of property right by a mere human. The more concrete demands of "Israelite" peasants probably involved some remembrances of earlier village communes. In Landsberger's words, "Goals will be more specific when past institutional structures can serve as a reference point, for example, the restoration of communal lands" (1969: 36). Finally, this

---

[24]Wolf (1966: 50–59) provides a convenient discussion of these terms as used here.

[25]Perhaps the two best attested examples are the *mir* of prerevolutionary Russia and *muša'a* tenure in the Near East (Wolf 1966: 78–79, 86, 90; Moore 1966: 475–76; Blum 1961: 510–12; Latron 1936: *passim*).

redistributional system of land tenure may provide one more reason why the earliest terrace-farmers in Israel grew cereals, rather than the grapes, olives, and nuts to which their hillside plots were better suited (see above, p. 50). For

> where a piece of land changes hands periodically, few cultivators will make permanent improvements on it. The system thus reinforces the traditional and relatively extensive cultivation of annual crops and discourages the introduction of intensively produced perennials (Wolf 1966: 79).

There is broad agreement that a final factor—outside leadership—not only favors organized peasant unrest, but is essential in transforming local peasant rebellions into broader agrarian revolt. "By themselves the peasants have never been able to accomplish a revolution. . . . They . . . have to have leaders from other classes" (Moore 1966: 479; cf. Landsberger 1973: 47–49; Wolf 1969: 294–96). *It is this factor, in the persons of the leaders of the Exodus group, which—along with the technological and demographic changes already noted—spells the difference between the peasant unrest patent in the Amarna letters and the broader revolt hypothesized as a crucial component in the formation of Israel as a society.* No matter who else was involved, the "Levites" of the earliest strata of biblical tradition have the strongest claim to this role, since a number of their names—including that of Moses—are Egyptian in etymology (Bright 1972: 119 and n. 28). Although the traditions concerning these premonarchic Levites are relatively sparse, they make reference to most of the characteristics which the leaders of peasant revolts are known to have exhibited.

The consciousness-arousing effects of military service for peasants were discussed above. A parallel break with traditional values would have been facilitated for future leaders by their living in a foreign country (Landsberger 1973: 27, 52; 1969: 41), in this case, sophisticated Egypt. In the biblical traditions of the Exodus from Egypt, the figure of Moses probably represents both the ideological fountainhead of later Israel and a generic composite of its leadership. As such, he manifests a related attribute frequent among the leaders and supporters of movements to change society, namely, "status inconsistency." This means that he is portrayed as ranking low in society according to one criterion, but high according to another: he was born a "Hebrew," but raised the son of Pharaoh's daughter. Lenski has articulated the cogent theory that the tensions and conflicts born of such inconsistent status often "lead individuals to react against the existing social order" (1966: 87; cf. 86–88, 288–89, 408–10).

The lineal and ideological descendents of the Moses group had potent seeds to sow and fertile soil in Canaan in which to sow them. As the root metaphor of their faith, they asserted that Yahweh had saved them from slavery by the defeat of Pharaoh and the elite of his troops. At Sinai, they believed, this same God had declared himself the only legitimate suzerain

and bound them to a covenantal blueprint for a just society.[26] If some of
the harried peasants of Palestine found this ideology and its bearers
appealing, they fit a common pattern:

> A peasantry which finds itself increasingly economically exploited by superior groups
> and institutions providing it no service in return, and with an ideology which provides
> no plausible justification for this, will be more susceptible to other ideal designs for
> society (Landsberger 1973: 40).

> Its leadership, particularly its outside leadership, imparts to peasant movements such
> ideologies as they have, particularly in the case of radical ideologies (Landsberger 1969:
> 52).

Nor did these outside leaders lack means of initiating their "Canaanite
converts" into the paradigmatic experiences of their faith. Although thinly
historicized and heavily encrusted with later accretions, Joshua 3–5 and 24
reflect at heart the liturgical recapitulation of the Exodus and Sinai events
in rites which instructed and incorporated new members, inculcated discipline and unity against the common enemy, and celebrated and reinforced
the power and legitimacy of their covenant with one another and with their
divine overlord. Both Gilgal and Shechem, the sites of these observances,
were broadly accessible from the frontier areas occupied by premonarchic
Israel.

   In the kind of goal-oriented organization here envisaged, however,
"the leader may be more prepared than his followers to use 'secondary'
violence as a premeditated means to vanquish the enemy, . . . or to unify
and animate a divided and sagging movement" (Landsberger 1969: 55).
"The adoption of violence as a means," moveover, "requires a paramilitary
type of organization" (Landsberger 1969: 55). Old traditions embedded in
Gen 34: 25–31; 49:5–7 and Exod 2:11–15; 32:25–29 cast Moses and the
Levites in just this mold.

   Such militancy and wide-ranging goals for the reconstruction of
society are not the only prerequisites of an organized movement. Networks
of communication are imperative, though necessarily difficult in a rural
setting (Landsberger 1969: 55–56). Without their bonding function, actions
cannot be coordinated, and the parochial interests and sectional jealousies
which typify peasant communities dissolve any larger unity or effectiveness.
Biblical tradition leaves little doubt that such centrifugal forces operated
powerfully in early Israel, and that most of the Israelite tribes constituted
separate cantons. The one conspicuous exception to this regionalism was
the Levites, who occupied no single area, but were spread as resident aliens

[26]Such statements, of course, presume some historical connection between Exodus and
Sinai—a matter much debated. Although far too complex to be rehearsed here, the issues and
literature have been surveyed recently for the interested reader (Nicholson 1973: 1–84; Campbell 1975: 141–51).

throughout the territories of the various other tribes (cf. Judg 17:7–9; 19:1). One may plausibly infer that, aided by the disarray of the upper classes in Canaan and the protection afforded by the terrain, they provided the loosely knit organization called Israel with both ideology and channels of communication in their role as non-elite priests. If so, they served a function frequently performed by members of the inferior clergy in other peasant revolts (Landsberger 1973: 49; Landsberger and Landsberger 1973: 123–24, 127–30; Lenski 1966: 263).

This brief attempt to delineate factors known on the basis of comparative investigation to foster significant agrarian revolt and to document their occurrence in the world of Israel's emergence has been far from exhaustive. It does suffice, however, to demonstrate that a model for the formation of ancient Israelite society which includes an element of peasant revolt fits established socio-historical parameters for agrarian societies and is not merely a romantic, modern fabrication, foisted without warrant upon the evidence.

The Revolt Model and Biblical Tradition

A final objection to such a model appeals to biblical tradition:

> The theory that Israel emerged from a Palestinian peasants' revolt finds no basis in the biblical materials, whether one considers the oldest discernible strata of the conquest tradition or the final canonical account. ... There is not the slightest hint in the biblical traditions regarding the revolution which supposedly brought Israel into existence. Surely one would expect to find some allusion to it in the book of Judges if such a revolution had in fact occurred (Miller 1977: 279; cf. Lapp 1967: 299).

While a full analysis of the biblical text in light of the revolt paradigm still remains to be undertaken, this working hypothesis *does* find support in the biblical materials as well as providing a plausible explanation for certain anomalies within the tradition. Only the briefest summary is possible here, but even it should serve to encourage the vigorous pursuit of such analysis rather than its a priori foreclosure.

That a connected narrative of a peasant revolt is not to be found in the Hebrew Bible can hardly occasion surprise. In their present form, virtually all OT narratives are the product of royal functionaries and/or priestly elites who could not be expected to transmit traditions of peasant uprisings in a sympathetic and unrefracted form. The "conquest" account in Joshua, as noted above, (p. 47), probably owes its present framework and orientation to the intense nationalism of the Josianic reform. From that perspective, "Canaan" and "Israel" were understandably viewed as nation-states and their conflict moralistically interpreted in terms of Deuteronomistic ideology. Even when the Deuteronomistic "mortar" and glosses are isolated on literary grounds (cf. n. 8, above) and bracketed, the older materials betray shaping from a number of different viewpoints, including that of the early monarchy (Noth 1953: 11–13; Tucker 1972: 71–86). Traditions more reflective of a revolt of the lower classes in Canaan have thus been abridged and muted, but not completely suppressed.

In the saga of Rahab the harlot in Joshua 2, for instance, only the first person plurals of the Deuteronomistic additions to Rahab's speech in vss. 9b–11 understand her as just another loyal subject of the king of Jericho, along with all "Canaanites" paralyzed with fear at the approach of large numbers of Israelite intruders. While the pre-Deuteronomistic remainder of the chapter has been truncated and edited, so that it abounds with tensions and unanswered questions, it basically reflects instead a conflict between the king and his retainers on the one side, and Rahab and the Israelite spies (or "messengers"; cf. Josh 6:17b, 25b) on the other. Nor can there be any question of the narrator's hostility toward the former or sympathy with the latter. These attitudes go far in placing the earlier narrator, his audience, and their enemies in terms of social roles and cleavages, the more so since characters in saga are often more generic than specific. Seen as such generic types, Rahab and the spies represent the urban lower classes and "outside agitators" against royal authority, respectively, for her "profession" places the harlot among the debased and vulnerable "expendables" of an agrarian city, while the Israelite representatives seek refuge in the hills (vss. 16, 22, 23), the traditional haven for anti-royal elements.[27] Not only would such groups not agonize over the morality of Rahab's lying or her means of subsistence, as have so many commentators since antiquity, but they would relish each repetition of the tale of her making an utter fool of the king. For the rest, the narrative emphasizes what would most concern the urban poor and those from outside who might seek to organize them. The former would require assurance that the movement would succeed (vss. 9a, 14b, 24a) and that they would survive the hostilities (vss. 12–14, 18–19); the latter would seek to guarantee that their secret plan not be exposed (vss. 14, 20–21). In short, the oldest kernal of the Rahab saga gives literary expression to one of the basic dynamics presumed by the revolt hypothesis, and would once have served to reinforce and legitimate the somewhat tenuous alliance between the groups typified by Rahab and the spies.

The literary linkage of this saga with the account in Joshua 6 of Jericho's fall is almost universally recognized as secondary, though pre-

---

[27]The socioeconomic role of prostitution in an agrarian city is well known (Lenski and Lenski 1978: 214–15; Sjoberg 1960: 134–37, 203–4). While Tucker (1972: 84) is correct that the present narrative does not specifically picture the spies enlisting a fifth column, "this business of ours" (vss. 14, 20) which they are so concerned not to have divulged can hardly have referred to anything else originally, for according to vss. 2–7, the king already knew of the presence of spies. In vs. 18, moreover, LXX has the spies speak of when they will enter "a part of the city." MT's bland reading of "the land" at this point is surely a secondary harmonization with Joshua 6. Note, too, the strategic location of Rahab's house in the city wall (vs. 15). Soggin (1972: 37–38) discusses these and other indications of what the current torso implies or presupposes, but does not state.

Deuteronomistic (Tucker 1972: 72). Compared with Joshua 2, chapter 6 exhibits quite a different genre. Like Joshua 3–4, its thin historicization poorly conceals liturgical origins (Cross 1973: 103–5, 138–44; Soggin 1972: 83, 86–88; see above, pp. 66–67). These origins, in turn, can account for the lack of remains from the "conquest" period at Jericho. Just as the march "from Shittim to Gilgal" (cf. Mic 6:5) could epitomize and celebrate escape from bondage, solemn procession around the nearby ruins of the ancient and once proud city of Jericho could symbolize the defeat of the elitist power (cf. Josh 6:2) manifested by *any* walled city (see above, p. 58). Jericho's role as the cultic archetype for the fall of the governing classes and the architectural expressions of their control would have been far less congenial to official celebrants and tradents of monarchic times, who could be expected to historicize this paradigmatic ritual into the miraculous capture of a specific enemy city.

As has long been noted, the Hebrew Bible contains no "conquest" narrative for much of central Palestine—a region marked in the Amarna period by the *ᶜapiru*-linked activities of Labaya. This area *is* represented in biblical tradition by accounts of covenants involving the Gibeonites (Josh 9–10) and Shechemites (Josh 24). Although these narratives have been embellished and refracted by any number of tradents and polemics, they seem at heart to reflect covenants between the "Israelites" and friendly "Canaanites" against the kings of Canaan (Wright 1962: 76–78). As Halpern has recently argued,

> . . . the Israelite treaties with Gibeon and Shechem may reflect the general process of defection by indigenous peoples from their aristocratic Canaanite overlords to an insurgent camp. Gibeon and Shechem, ruled by their elders, chose to make common cause with the Israelite invaders against the monarchs of Jerusalem and other towns. In so doing, they gave expression to Canaan's social cleavage. The imperial towns of the coastal plain and trade routes could no longer enforce their will in the central hills (1975: 312).

That the dynasts of Canaan were the primary targets of such alliances is also suggested by the list of defeated kings in Joshua 12 (Mendenhall 1973: 26). While some of the specifics of this list may date to the Solomonic period (Fritz 1969: 136–61), the underlying genre and much of the information are "certainly very ancient" (Soggin 1972: 143). Rather than picturing the capture and annihilation of whole cities, this list names the kings— many of whose cities are specifcally mentioned elsewhere as untaken— whose power to control the countryside has been effectively neutralized and whose lands may accordingly be alloted to "Israelites." In this regard, the situation presumed is an accelerated version of that mirrored in the Amarna letters.

Although all these diverse materials from the book of Joshua lend at least circumstantial support to the revolt model, the prose of each has been heavily and repeatedly redacted, leaving the evidence more ambiguous than a modern historian might wish. The relatively unrevised poetry of the Song of Deborah in Judges 5 takes on added significance in this context, for not only is its claim to predate the monarchy more widely recognized in critical scholarship than that of any other composition in the Hebrew Bible, but its subject is the conflict between Israel and the kings of Canaan. Long before Mendenhall's article of 1962, scholars sought to exploit this unusually direct access to the struggle. Already in the 19th century, Moore drew the following conclusions from his circumspect analysis of Judges 5:

> The Canaanite city-kings of these [Taanach and Megiddo] and neighboring cities, relying on their chariots and their superiority in arms, gave battle in the open field. . . . The Israelites . . . were peasants from the hills, and were armed only with peasants' weapons; a regular military equipment was hardly to be found among them" (1895: 134–35).

From the sociological side, Weber also recognized the relationship between topography and social stratification:

> In the fertile plains and on the coast, the military patrician of the cities was the enemy against whom . . . the mountain peasant . . . had to fight. . . .

> The peasant proprietor was the main champion of the battle against the urban patrician. He was most exposed to the imposition of forced labor. The Deborah war was conducted essentially as a peasant war. Praised most highly by the Song is the fact that untrained mountain footmen have fought . . . and have been victorious (1952: 54–55).

A more recent study by the present writer (Chaney 1976: *passim*) reaches similar conclusions and seeks to demonstrate in detail that such an understanding of the conflict consistently applied also aids in solving many of the song's textual and philological puzzles.

If these passages from Joshua and Judges ultimately derive from various stages of a protracted struggle between the kings of Canaan and "Israelite" peasants, as suggested, the narratives about David in I Samuel 23–27; 29–30 depict a logical sequel. By David's time, most of the old Canaanite city-states were part of a Philistine-Canaanite symbiosis under the far more efficient control of a military aristocracy. The Philistine tyrants who had filled the vacuum in political power were unwilling to allow the central hill country a continuance of its separate ways, for its growing peasant population had become an economic base worth exploiting. Utilizing military tactics more appropriate to the uplands, the Philistines sought to subjugate and garrison Israel. Under such circumstances, Israel's unconsolidated peasant revolution partially reverted to the prerevolutionary level of "social banditry" represented by David's "Hebrew" band (see below, p. 83). The unstable conditions, in turn, allowed David, the master strategist, to translate this nucleus of power into an agrarian monarchy.

But aspects of the monarchic state which he founded deviated significantly from the norm for agrarian societies—deviations which find plausible explanation in the reconstruction of premonarchic Israel sketched here. Law is one such area. Since the laws of the Pentateuch exhibit detailed affinities in both form and content with the legal tradition preserved in cuneiform sources, the comparison of Israelite jurisprudence with that typical of other ancient Near Eastern societies can be particularly nuanced (Greenberg 1962: 733–44; Paul 1970: 36–42). These commonalities also serve to make the contrasts all the more stark. Whereas the collections of cuneiform law "are the product of a secular jurisprudence which recognized the state and the king as the promulgators and ultimate sanction of the law" (Greenberg 1962: 737), Yahweh is conceived as the *sole* fountainhead of biblical law, and he "selects the entire corporate body of Israel to be the recipients of his law" (Paul 1970: 38). That law rejects any class distinctions in meting out justice. For the cuneiform legal corpora, "social status is decisive in evaluating harms and assessing penalties" (Greenberg 1962: 737). "Biblical law [also] diverges from other law systems of the ancient Near East in not regarding any offense against property as a capital crime" (Greenberg 1962: 734). In the case of a runaway slave, cuneiform laws seek to protect the owner, with the crime of harboring such a fugitive sometimes punishable by death (cf. Laws of Lipit-Ishtar 12–13; Laws of Eshnunna 49–52; Laws of Hammurabi 15–20; Hittite Laws 22–24). Deut 23:15–16 (Heb. 16–17), by contrast, *mandates* this harboring and the unprejudiced incorporation of the runaway into the community. No typical agrarian monarch could countenance such a policy, not to speak of promulgating it. At the court of Solomon, for instance, the right of a master to reclaim runaway slaves was a foregone conclusion (cf. I Kgs 2:39–40). It has long been recognized, however, that biblical law did not originate with the monarchic state of Israel; it had premonarchic roots in town and village institutions which continued to function alongside royal administrative structures (Noth 1966: 1–107; Mendenhall 1954: 26–46; Köhler 1956: 127–50). Both the grassroots tenacity and the anomalous content of this legal tradition find cogent explication in the revolt model for Israel's emergence as a society. The polemically deviant ideals which inform Pentateuchal law—God as the sole sanction of the law and all of the people as its recipient, no recognition of class distinctions, rights of persons placed above those of property, and the duty to provide sanctuary and communal inclusion to any fugitive from elite power—are readily intelligible as those of peasant revolutionaries and their leaders. The two contending models do not plausibly explain these anomalies, or even address the issue of their causation.

Israelite prophecy may be viewed in much the same light. While it, too, had antecedents and parallels in the other societies of the ancient Near East, its critique of agrarian monarchy and its concomitants were unprecedentedly vigorous. Particularly scathing invectives were directed

toward wealthy landlords and creditors who pressed sharp marketing and
foreclosure procedures against previously freeholding peasants, thereby
concentrating land ownership in a few hands and creating a large mass of
landless cultivators (Alt 1959: 348–72). The canons against which the
prophets measured these practices were essentially those of the legal
tradition just discussed, and like it, they are more fully explained by a
heritage ultimately derived from a process of peasant revolt.

In sum, biblical tradition supports the revolt model in two ways.
Despite the work of later redactors and editors, it contains numerous
allusions to conflicts and dynamics in premonarchic times of the type
envisaged by this gestalt. Other traditions evidence a marked departure
from more typical agrarian patterns by certain of monarchic Israel's
institutions. The revolt model provides a plausible explanation for these
mutations; the contending hypotheses do not.

CONCLUSIONS

As paradigms for the formation of premonarchic Israel as a separate
society in Palestine, the models of nomadic infiltration and conquest by a
large group of intruders both proceed from assumptions which appear
fundamentally flawed. While it remains a working hypothesis, a model of
peasant and frontier revolt has been found to accomodate an illuminate the
data provided by the Amarna archive. Syro-Palestinian archaeology, and
the biblical tradition, and to do so within parameters defined by the
comparative study of agrarian societies by social scientists. Its heuristic
value alone argues that this model and its sociologically derived research
strategies be tested in greater detail against each of the sets of relevant data.
The writer will consider this paper a success if it serves to enlist new
recruits in that ongoing process.[28]

EXCURSUS

THE ʿApiru AND SOCIAL UNREST IN THE
AMARNA LETTERS FROM SYRO-PALESTINE

Perhaps the fullest account of social unrest preserved in the Amarna
archive was written by the prolific Rib-Adda of Byblos. It can serve to
focus our discussion.

---

[28]The issue of the *Journal for the Study of the Old Testament* containing discussion of the
"peasants' revolt" hypothesis by Hauser (1978a: 2–19; 1978b: 35–36), Thompson (1978: 20–
27), Mendenhall (1978: 28–34), and Gottwald (1978a: 37–52) appeared after the current article
had been accepted for publication. While revision to make direct reference to that discussion
is thus precluded, it will be obvious that many of the issues raised there are anticipated and
explicitly addressed here.

All my towns which are in the mountains and on the seashore have joined with the
ᶜapiru troops. Byblos, together with (only) two towns, remains in my possession. And
behold, now, Abdi-Ashirta has take Shigata for himself and said to the people of
Ammia: "Kill your leader! Then you will be like us and you will have peace." So they
acted according to his words and they are like ᶜapiru. And behold, now, Abdi-Ashirta
has written to the troops: "Assemble in Bit-NIN.URTA and let us fall upon Byblos!
Behold, there is no one who will save it from our hand! So let us drive out the
'governors' from the midst of the lands, and let an alliance be formed for all the lands,
and then sons and daughers will have peace forever! And if, indeed, the king (of Egypt)
does come out, then all lands will be hostile to him, so what can he do to us?" Thus
they exchanged oaths. And thus I am very, very fearful because there is no one who
will rescue me from their hand (*EA* 74: 19–45).[29]

There can be no doubt of Abdi-Ashirta's opportunistic manipulation of the
situation, but his program is unintelligible without widespread unrest
among the lower classes to be manipulated.[30] In the same vein, while Rib-
Adda clearly desired to vilify a political adversary to the Egyptian court,
his proclivity elsewhere for the use of vague slurs to convince Pharaoh of
the anti-Egyptian import of Abdi-Ashirta's activities renders this report on
specific tactics all the more trustworthy. Such extended reflection on the
concerns of the non-elite majority, albeit only in an elite-held mirror, is
understandably rare in the diplomatic correspondence of Amarna. Even so,
all major aspects of this one, somewhat fuller account are echoed more
briefly in other letters.

Time and again the petty dynasts of the city-states, regularly called
"governors" (*ḫazannūtu*) in the letters, feared assassination, mostly by the
lower classes of their own people. Rib-Adda wrote of it repeatedly with
regard to himself and other dynasts (in addition to the passages quoted, see
also *EA* 75:25–34; 82:33–45; 89:10–32; 130:31–33; 131:18–30; 132:43–50;
138:9–14; 139:12–15, 33–40; 140:10–14):

And all the "governors" seek to have this done to Abdi-Ashirta [to have archer troops
advance from Egypt so that Abdi-Ashirta's people, following the greatest might, will
defect to the "governors'" side] because he wrote to the people of Ammia: "Kill your
lord!" And they joined with the ᶜapiru. So the "governors" are saying: "Thus he will do
to us, and all the lands will join with the ᶜapiru (*EA* 73:23–33)."

Byblos and Batruna (alone) remain mine, and he [Abdi-Ashirta] seeks to take (these)
two cities. He has also said to the people of [Batruna]: "Kill your lord!" And they have
joined with the ᶜapiru, like the city of Ammia (*EA* 81: 9–13).

[29]This translation presupposes the readings and interpretations advanced by Mendenhall
(1947: 123–24) and Moran (1953: 78–80, esp. nn. 4 and 5). The rendering of *ālu* in 11.19 and
22 as "town" cannot adequately represent the word's range: "city-town-village" (*AHw*: 39;
CAD, vol. 1: 379–88). That *EA* lacks a separate word for "village" is frequently germane to
the discussion which follows.

[30]This is also the explicit and unequivocal conclusion of Artzi (1964: 165–66). It is
difficult to understand how Weippert (1971: 74, n. 72) can cite Artzi as being in basic
agreement with him.

I fear the peasants (awīlūt ḫu-u[p-ši]), that they will slay me (EA 77:36–37).[31]

Nor was such activity limited to Syria; it is witnessed for Palestine as well. Abdu-Heba of Jerusalem narrated the following events, also reported in EA 335:7–20.

> . . . but now ʿapiru hold the cities of the king. There is not one "governor" (left) to the king, my lord—all are lost! Behold, Turbazu has been slain in the (very) gate of Sile, (yet) the king is negligent. Behold, (as for) Zimrida of Lachish,[32] slaves/servants who had become ʿapiru smote him. Yaptih-Adda has been slain in the (very) gate of Sile, (yet) the king is negligent. Wherefore does the king not call them to task (EA 288:36–47)?

Milkilu of Gezer encountered analogous problems:

> Let the king, my lord, know that the hostility against me and against Shuwardata is powerful. So let the king, my lord, deliver his land from the hand of the ʿapiru. If not, let the king, my lord, send chariots to fetch us, that our slaves/servants not slay us (EA 271:9–21)!

According to Baʿlat-UR.MAḪ^MEŠ of Sapuna, the threat extended to Milkilu's sons, who probably represented his authority in the towns named:

[31]Note the threat of the ʿapiru in 11.21–35 (partially broken). While ḫupšu will regularly be translated here as "peasants," the larger interpretation being argued does not depend upon the exact equivalence of the two terms. As a matter of fact, the English term is so difficult of sociologically precise definition that no two scholars can agree upon its exact limits or essentials, prompting Landsberger's cogent recommendation (1973: 6–18) that the term cover the continuum of "all low-status cultivators" who constitute the large majority of any agrarian society. "Peasants" in that sense translates ḫupšu well, for the latter are seen in various contexts as present in large numbers, holding small, rural plots, lacking significant property, and being subject to corvée and military service (Wiseman 1953: 10; Weippert 1971: 72, n. 63; Dietrich, Loretz, and Sanmartín 1974: 26–27; and the literature there cited). In some of the Amarna passages, the latter sense—"peasant troops"—may be primary.

As usually translated, EA 112:10–12 would also constitute succinct proof that Rib-Adda faced both external hostility and internal rebellion by the lower classes of his own people:

> From whom shall I protect myself? From my enemies or from my peasants (awīlūt ḫu-up-ši-ia)?

Moran (1975: 154, 165, n. 68) has recently argued persuasively, however, that ištu means "with" in this and other passages in peripheral Akkadian, and that the lines are therefore ironical:

> With whom shall I protect myself? With my enemies or with my peasants?!

The context of the other passages quoted makes obvious why Rib-Adda could expect as little aid from his peasants as from his enemies, but it is unclear here whether the main thrust of his rhetoric is that his peasants would be unwilling or unable to mount a defense comparable to that of the garrison which he once enjoyed and for whose return he now pleads.

[32]Zi-im-ri-da ^URU L[a-k]i-si^ki is translated here casus pendens. For a partial parallel, cf. EA 75:25–29.

Let the king, my lord, know that hostility is practiced in the land and that the land of the king, my lord, is gone through desertion to the ᶜapiru. So let the king, my lord, attend to his land, and let the king, my lord, know that ᶜapiru sent word to Aijalon and to Zorah, and the two sons of Milkilu were nearly slain (*EA* 273:8–24).

A letter of undetermined origin strikes a similar note:

Let the king, my lord, know that the "governors," who were in the city of my lord, have come to an end and all the land of the king, my lord, has deserted to the ᶜapiru (*EA* 272:10–17).

Rib-Adda bemoaned desertion and internal rebellion by the lower classes often (in addition to the passages quoted, see also *EA* 69:12–28; 91:14–15; 104:37–45; 125:25–30):

What should I do? Behold, they kill the "governors." There *are* no cities. They are like dog(s), and there is no one who seeks after them. What should I do, I, who dwell amidst ᶜapiru? If now I have no provisions of the king, then my peasants (*awīlūt ḫu-up-ši-ia*) will become hostile.[33] All lands are inimical to me (*EA* 130:30–43).

So let the king concern himself about his city and his servant, for my peasants (*awīlūt ḫu-* [!] *ši-ia*) seek to desert (*EA* 114:20–22).

The relation between such desertion and the "taking" of cities and lands[34] is tersely delineated in two passages:

Hostility is powerful against me, and there are no provisions for the peasants (*awīlūt ḫu-pu-ši*), so therefore they desert to the sons of Abdi-Ashirta and to Sidon and to Beirut. Truly, the sons of Abdi-Ashirta are hostile to the king, and Sidon and Beirut no longer belong to the king. Send a commissioner that he may seize them. Let him not abandon the city and go off to you. Truly, if the peasants (*awīlūt ḫu-up-ši*) desert, the ᶜapiru will capture the city (*EA* 118:21–39).

Now I am guarding the towns of Byblos, the city of the king, night and day. If I should (attempt to) conquer the lands, then the men would desert in order to take lands for themselves, and there would be no men to guard Byblos, the city of the king, my lord. So may my lord hastily despatch archer-troops or we die (*EA* 362:31–42).

While the latter passage does not specifically mention ᶜapiru, it does name the ᶜapiru-linked sons of Abdi-Ashirta (1. 67) and refer ominously to activities characteristic of ᶜapiru with the indefinite "they" of several verbal forms. The picture is that of an agrarian elite clinging fearfully to its erod-

---

[33]Unfortunately, both the reading of the verb and its meaning involve some uncertainty. The translation here presumes *ul-ta-na*[-*n*]*a*, understood as a Dt of *šanānu* (cf. Knudtzon 1915: 555, n. f; Ebeling *apdu* Knudtzon 1915: 1394–95; *AHw*: 1116a; Rainey 1970: 81).

[34]ᶜApiru are said to be involved in "taking" towns and cities in *EA* 71:10–32; 76:7–20; 79:7–29; 81:6–13; 90:5–25; 91:13–26; 185:9–64; 288: 36–46; 289:5–24. They "take" land in 76:7–20; 83:15–20; 289:5–24.

ing power base, while finding it impossible to control the cultivated country-side or its popualtion.[35]

Given an opportunity, the lower classes of the cities—some of whom were probably peasants who had forcibly urbanized due to hostilities (cf. *EA* 81:33–41; 85:10–15)—also deserted to other leaders, whose promised programs had greater appeal, and thereby "joined with" *ᶜapiru*:

> . . . so I cannot go out (of Bylos) or Byblos would join with *ᶜapiru*. They [Rib-Adda's enemies mentioned earlier in the letter] came to Ibirta, and an agreement was made with *ᶜapiru* (*EA* 104: 49–54; for *epēšu pû*, see *CAD*, Vol. 4: 216).
>
> . . . the hostility is powerful against me. I fear my peasants (*ḫu-up-ši-ia*). So I have written to the palace for a garrison and men of Meluha. . . . Let the king send garrison troops and men of Meluha to guard me, lest the city join with the *ᶜapiru* (*EA* 117:89–94).

In another instance, this time from the Esdraelon valley, the people of Taanach "took" their own city in the manner counseled by Abdi-Ashirta's speech in *EA* 74, "driving out" their "governor" and attacking his privileged property:[36]

> Let the king, my lord, know that the people of Taanach have moved to attack every last thing which the king, my lord, has given to his servant, and they have butchered my cattle and driven me out! And behold, I am staying with Biridiya ["governor" of nearby Megiddo], and let the king, my lord, care for his servant (*EA* 248:9–22).

Even though *ᶜapiru* are not explicitly named in Yashdata's account of the revolt, they do appear as the enemies of Biridiya (*EA* 243:19–22; 246:5–10), with whom Yashdata was closely allied and identified (*EA* 245:11–18). The social dynamics are, in any case, more important than the particular term applied to the group involved, for the nameless masses who "join with, become, desert to," or "are like" *ᶜapiru*, or who otherwise side with them, are variously characterized as "peoples, lands, cities, peasants," and "slaves," with more than one designation often used within a few lines of the same letter.[37]

---

[35]Both Sjoberg (1960; esp. 80–144) and Lenski and Lenski (1978: 186–87, 201–15) delineate the predominantly urban base of agrarian elites and their relationship to the rural population.

[36]While it is nowhere explicitly stated that Yashdata, the writer of *EA* 248, was "governor" of Taanach, no other assumption adequately explains the contents of this letter and Yashdata's relationship to Biridya of Megiddo (Helck 1962: 189). Note that forms of *dubburu* are used both here and in *EA* 74:34 for the "driving out" or "expulsion" of "governors."

[37]For "people" joining with, being like, or wholly going over to the *ᶜapiru*, see *EA* 73:26–29; 74:25–29; 81:11–13 (all quoted above); and 179:20–22; cf. 121:19–23. "Lands" joining with, being lost to, or deserting to the *ᶜapiru* are mentioned in *EA* 73:32–33; 74:35–36 (both quoted above); 76:33–37; 77:26–29; 79:18–26; 85:69–74; 88:29–34; 111:17–21; 117:56–58; 148:45; 215:9–17; 272:14–17; 273:11–14 (quoted above); and 290:12–13. "Cities" join with or are lost to the *ᶜapiru* in 68:12–18; 74:19–21 (quoted above); 76:33–37; 81:11–13 (quoted

Many of the elements in this fluidity and complexity can be delineated and integrated within Hobsbawm's conceptualization of "social banditry" (1965: 13–29; 1969: 11–115; 1973: 142–57). His broadly comparative studies of this phenomenon have not previously been applied to the *apiru* problem, but such application is suggested by the common description of at least some *apiru* as brigands. Both Weippert's careful rendering of "outlaws" for the non-Amarna *apiru* (1971: 58–65) and Rowton's useful discussion of the "parasocial element" (1977: 181–98) grant initial encouragement. Closer comparison reveals significant congruities between Amarna's *apiru* and social banditry. The latter

> . . . consists essentially of relatively small groups of men living on the margins of peasant society, and whose activities are considered criminal by the prevailing official power-structure and value-system, but not (or not without strong qualification) by the peasantry (Hobsbawm 1973: 143; cf. Mendenhall 1973: 130–35).

A "remarkably uniform . . . phenomenon throughout the ages and continents" (Hobsbawm 1969: 11), social banditry "is found throughout the wide belt of rural societies which lies between the tribally organized and the modern industrial, excepting only, it would seem, formalized caste societies" (Hobsbawm 1973: 148). "Otherwise social bandity is universally found, wherever societies are based on agriculture (including pastoral economies), and consist largely of peasants and landless labourers ruled, oppressed and exploited by someone else" (Hobsbawm 1969: 15).

Hobsbawm's description of those who became social bandits and of the ambiguity of their relationship to constituted authority is not only reminiscent of the Amarna *apiru*, it also aids the analysis of their often crosscut role(s). "If we want to understand the social composition of banditry," he writes, "we must . . . look primarily at the mobile margin of peasant society" (Hobsbawm 1969: 25). "The overwhelming majority of the normal brigands were peasants, herdsmen or—what comes to the same thing—ex-soldiers" (Hobsbawm 1965: 29). Whether escaped serfs, ruined freeholders, pastoralists denied access to sufficient pasturage, or low-ranking servicemen who had been discharged or had deserted, they all shared an economic marginality and official opprobrium, without having

---

above); 104:51–52 (quoted above); 116:37–38; 117:92–94 (quoted above); 144:24–33; and 207:19–21; cf. 87:18–24; 88:29–34; and 189:9–18. Slaves/servants are said to have become *apiru* in 288:44, while "peasants" (*ḫupšu*) are linked with *apiru* in EA 77:21–37; 117:89–94; 118:21–37; 130:30–43 (all quoted above). Although some of the briefer passages cited might be understood as referring primarily to political rebellion against Egypt, the revolt of the lower and peripheral elements of the city-state societies against their top and center as personified in the "governor" is clear in the fuller texts quoted. Because of the linkage between the political and socioeconomic factors, they cannot be neatly distinguished either in the language of the letters or in the underlying reality. Sparser contexts, however, should be read in light of the more amply attested evidence.

violated the values and norms of the groups from which they constituted "seepage," and whose continued empathy they enjoyed (Hobsbawm 1969: 27; for "seepage" cf. Rowton 1967a: 14–15). If the Amarna ᶜapiru are viewed in this light, the widespread sympathy which they found in the countryside and the constant threat that the ḫupšu—viewed in either their socioeconomic or military role—would desert to them are both easily understood.

An assumption that many of the Amarna texts reflect social banditry also allows the unstrained interpretation of links between ᶜapiru and portions of the non-peasant population. "Since the bandits' fundamental loyalty was to peasants, with their permanent opposition to the actual authorities, even the most traditionalist brigand had no difficulty in making common cause with other oppositionists and revolutionaries, especially if they were also persecuted" (Hobsbawm 1965: 28–29). The ability of this paradigm thus to integrate the social unrest and political opportunism witnessed in the texts extends to a phenomenon evidenced in a letter from Yapahu of Gezer:

> Let the king, my lord, know that my youngest brother is estranged from me, and has entered Muhhazu, and has made an agreement with (lit.: "given his two hands to"; see Greenberg 1955: 49) an ᶜapiru (EA 298:20–27).

Hobsbawm has written appositely that "where landowning families fight and feud, make and break family alliances, dispute heritages with arms, the stronger accumulating wealth and influence over the broken bones of the weaker, the scope for bands of fighting men led by the disgruntled losers is naturally very large" (1969: 82). Such disaffected or impoverished nobles easily adopt the bandit's life because "arms are their privilege, fighting their vocation and the basis of their systems of values" (Hobsbawm 1969: 30).

In specifying the conditions which tend to multiply bandits, Hobsbawm could hardly have described Late Bronze Canaan more aptly:

> The ideal situation for robbery is one in which the local authorities are local men, operating in complex local situations, and where a few miles may put the robber beyond the reach or even the knowledge of one set of authorities and into the territory of another, which does not worry about what happened 'abroad' (1969: 17).

One is reminded of the protests of Mayarzana of Hazi (EA 185; 186) that Amanhatbi of Tushulti consistently harbored ᶜapiru after they harrassed and plundered Mayarzana's territory. Situations "where the central state apparatus is absent or ineffective and the regional centres of power are balanced or unstable, as in conditions of 'feudal anarchy', in frontier zones, among a shifting mosaic of petty principalities" (Hobsbawm 1969: 82), foster banditry. So do harvest failures—whether due to natural causes or the disruption of cultivation by hostilities (cf. EA 74:17–19; 75:10–17; 81:33–41; 90:36–44)—and wars, both of which reduce the peasant's economic viability (Hobsbawm 1969: 18).

In such chaotic circumstances, a robber band, even though it is relatively small, constitutes a political force, because it forms a nucleus of armed strength.

> Where the state is remote, ineffective and weak, it will indeed be tempted to come to terms with any local power-group it cannot defeat. If robbers are successful enough, they have to be conciliated just like any other centre of armed force (Hobsbawm 1969: 44; cf. 1973: 156).

Such considerations surely functioned in the Egyptian crown's failure to respond with alacrity to the "governors'" repeated appeals for campaigns against the *ᶜapiru* in their region. That even Abdi-Ashirta's recognition by the Egyptian state (*EA* 101:29–31) represented something of this dynamic is suggested by Rib-Adda's fulminations.

> What is Abdi-Ashirta, the slave, the dog, that he takes the land of the king himself? What is his auxiliary force, that it should be strong? (Only) by means of *ᶜapiru* is his auxiliary force strong! So send me fifty teams of horses and 200 infantrymen in order that I may resist him in Shigata (*EA* 71:20-26).

Furthermore, as noted by Mendenhall (1973: 123), none of the six letters of Abdi-Ashirta or the eleven of his son, Aziru, ever mentions the term *ᶜapiru*—a fact which places them in a distinct minority at Amarna. Were these leaders sensitive about their origins?

A paradigm of social banditry also allows the Amarna *ᶜapiru* to be related plausibly to the use of the term in other texts. "Elsewhere they are settled in cities, serving in the armies of states or supported by private individuals—in all cases a recognized element in society" (Greenberg 1955: 76). The difference lies in the relative strength or weakness of centralized authority, for "retainers, policemen, mercenary soldiers are . . . often recruited from the same material as social bandits" (Hobsbawm 1965: 13; cf. 1969: 61–62). Those elements who became the "landlords' bandits" and the "states' bandits" in more settled times and places were propelled into "social banditry" by the anarchy of Syro-Palestine in the Amarna Age.

A profound ambiguity, however, was inherent in this new role.

> For the crucial fact about the bandit's social situation is its ambiguity. He is an outsider and a rebel, a poor man who refuses to accept the normal roles of poverty, and establishes his freedom by means of the only resources within reach of the poor, strength, bravery, cunning, and determination. This draws him close to the poor: he is one of them. It sets him in opposition to the hierarchy of power, wealth and influence: he is not one of them. . . . At the same time the bandit is, inevitably, drawn into the web of wealth and power, because, unlike other peasants, he acquires wealth and exerts power. He is 'one of us' who is constantly in the process of becoming associated with 'them'. The more successful he is as a bandit, the more he is *both* a representative and champion of the poor *and* a part of the system of the rich (Hobsbawm 1969: 76).

The Amarna *ᶜapiru* are better served by recognition of this intrinsic ambiguity than by attempts to force them into a straitjacket of political, social, or lexicographical consistency.

In quantitative terms, too, the Syro-Palestinian ᶜapiru fit Hobsbawm's picture of social banditry. Brigand bands are normally small, "larger operations being undertaken by coalitions of such groups" (Hobsbawm 1973: 155; cf. 1965: 18–19). Despite images of nomadic hordes or massive military operations conjured up by some discussions of the Amarna ᶜapiru, the specific information provided by the letters themselves points to bands of modest size. One of these is said to have had forty survivors after action in which some of its members were killed (EA 185:42–49). The requests of the "governors" for special, outside forces to control the ᶜapiru are often for less than 100 men and never more than 400 (on 132:56–57, see Pintore 1972: 103, n. 9). Only at Byblos do the numbers exceed 200 (Greenberg 1955: 75; Campbell 1960: 21; Pintore 1972: 101–31; 1973: 299–318). Since the bands appear to have operated from rugged terrain with a sparse but sympathetic population, the conventional troops needed to control them effectively would have outnumbered the ᶜapiru themselves. Greenberg's conclusion that they usually roamed and raided "in groups of perhaps 50–100 men" (1955: 75) is therefore well within the evidence. Such figures lend support to Mendenhall's observation that, for all the rhetoric of the letters, very few cities are reported actually to have been captured in battle by ᶜapiru troops (1973: 126, 129; cf. Campbell 1960: 21). Far from the clash of major armies, the process reflected is rather the harassment and intrigue typical of bandits operating with the sympathy of those social elements from which they sprang. The somewhat larger troop requests, moreover, came from Rib-Adda of Byblos, whose letters contain explicit references to alliances with or among the ᶜapiru (EA 74:36–37, 42; 104:52–54). While the Egyptian court chose to acknowlege the strength of the coalitions formed, it did so, not by sending the troop contingents for which Rib-Adda continually begged, but by granting de facto legitimacy to forces which it could not control, at least, not at a cost deemed reasonable.

Hobsbawm's analysis illumines the nature of the "governors'" pleas for troops and mercenaries from Egypt as well as the numbers involved, for he states as a general principle what the letters illustrate so profusely: at the local and sometimes even regional level, "everybody has to come to terms with large and well-established bandits" (Hobsbawm 1969: 78). The compromised stance in which local officials thus inevitably find themselves "explains why in really bandit-infested areas campaigns against banditry are so often carried out by special forces brought in from the outside" (Hobsbawm 1969: 79).

Geographic factors, however, usually work against the outsiders. "For obvious reasons" social banditry "has always flourished best in remote and inaccessible areas (e.g., mountains, forests . . .), and under inefficient administration" (Hobsbawm 1973: 149; cf. 1969: 16, 61, 79, 82). We have already noted Rowton's argument that the ᶜapiru of Syro-Palestine operated in and from such terrain, where the chariots of the elite were disadvantaged (1965: 375–87; 1976b: 29–30). Further illustration may be found in *EA* 292, in which Baal-Shipti of Gezer writes that "there is hostility towards me from the mountains" (11. 28–29), and alludes to paying brigands a standard price of thirty pieces of silver to ransom someone "from the mountians" (11. 48–50).

In similar regions elsewhere, "where agents of authority enter only on occasional forays, the bandit may actually live in the village" (Hobsbawm 1969: 39). "Indeed in the real back country, . . . the bandit may be not only tolerated and protected, but a leading member of the community". . . (Hobsbawm 1969: 40). The latter statement does not accord ill with the picture of Labaya and his sons which the letters afford (cf. *EA* 243:19–22 with 244:8–33; 246 rev. 5–10; 250; 253; 254; 287:29–31; 289:5–29). Their *ᶜapiru*-associated activities radiated out from the thinly settled, mountainous region around Shechem at least as far as the territory of Megiddo, Gezer, and Jerusalem. One gains the impression that they moved about the wooded uplands with impunity, prompting some of the "governors" into uneasy and shifting alliances with them. Although Labaya can write grandiloquently of his fealty to Pharaoh when he is explaining away his relative's involvement with *ᶜapiru* (*EA* 254:31–46), the truculent tone and barbarous language of *EA* 252 express the backwoods independence which he really enjoyed in his mountain domain.

Finally, it may be observed that philological obscurity and semantic ambiguity are characteristic of the terminology applied to social bandits (Hobsbawm 1965: 21; 1969: 61; 1973: 154–56). The orthography of the letters makes this doubly true of *ᶜapiru*, for not only is the etymology mooted, as seen above, but the ideogram SA. GAZ and its variants, by which *ᶜapiru* is represented in a large majority of its occurrences, also represents Akkadian *ḫabbātu*, "robber, bandit, raider" (Rowton 1965: 386; 1976a: 14–15; Greenberg 1955: 88–90). We have noted as well that ambiguity is inherent both within the social role described and in the expansion of the term in political name-calling. Even when *ᶜapiru* was not being used by one "governor" merely to malign another, however, the ambiguity of the social phenomenon designated was matched by the variety of social perspectives from which it was viewed and evaluated, and these differences were reflected in the use of language. Because most of the letters were written by the ruling elite of the city-states, Hobsbawm's remark that "bandit" has "become a habitual term . . . governments use to describe revolutionary guerrillas" (1965: 21), has significance for the identity of at least some *ᶜapiru*. (Note once again that Abdi-Ashirta and Aziru eschewed any use of the term.)

Since Hobsbawm's delineation of social banditry has proven apt in analyzing many of the intricacies of Amarna's *ᶜapiru*, his understanding of the relationship between such activities and broader peasant movements warrants exploration. By itself, "banditry is not so much a form of peasant movement as a symptom of peasant unrest" (Hobsbawm 1973: 153), but it "may be regarded as a precursor, and a primitive form of, wider peasant agitations" (Hobsbawm 1973: 146). Hobsbawm sees three kinds of relationship between the terms.

"*First*, banditry and more ambitious types of peasant movement tend to flourish in the same areas, if not actually to live in symbiosis" (Hobsbawm 1973: 146). In the Amarna Age, it was the hinterlands of Palestine and Syria—particularly those in the mountains—which spawned and harbored both ᶜapiru bands and more broadly based movements against the "governors." The Israelites later occupied the Palestinian portion of this zone and had the dynasts of the same Canaanite city-states as enemies. Concurrent with the appearance of premonarchic Israel in Palestine, technological developments made the traditional areas of resistance to these kings' authority economically viable for a much larger population. That the poor, unwalled, "Israelite" towns and villages which came to dot the old ᶜapiru territory were peopled by peasants who had revolted is not thereby proven, but it is rendered plausible in the absence of cogent hypothesis or definite evidence to the contrary.

"*Second*, at times when mass unrest grips the peasantry, banditry merges with these larger movements, and notable increases in banditry may indeed prepare and announce them" (Hobsbawm 1973: 146). Such a merger appears to be reflected in at least some of the declarations that "peasants, slaves, peoples, lands," and "cities" "join with, become," and "desert to" the ᶜapiru. It also reconciles the reports of large-scale participation by these groups in ᶜapiru-like activities with the relatively small size of the ᶜapiru bands proper. As any student of the comparative study of peasant movement knows, however, "the more extensive and . . . permanent the movement becomes, the less likely it is to be, or at least remain, in the hands of peasants" (Landsberger 1973: 47). Abdi-Ashirta and Aziru, for instance, seem to have manipulated the widespread social unrest in their region much as they played the Egyptian and Hittite empires against one another—toward their own opportunistic ends. Thus, when Hittite power was able to intervene decisively in the area, it "plucked with little difficulty the fruits of the SA.GAZ movement" (Mendenhall 1973: 129). No comparable interruption of the ferment in Palestine is known. With regard to notable increases in banditry preparing and announcing larger movements, we need add to the picture of rampant ᶜapiru outlawry already sketched only that still other Amarna letters speak of the harassment and interdiction of caravans in Syro-Palestine (*EA* 7:73–82; 8:13–41; 16:37–42; 148:20–23; 255:8–25; 264:5–25).

"*Third*, banditry may itself provide the model or cadre of certain kinds of primitive peasant insurrection or guerrilla activity" (Hobsbawm 1973: 147). Particularly "likely is the systematic use of bandit tactics and experience for the technically very similar activities of guerrilla warfare" (Hobsbawm 1973: 147). In that sense, the letters speak accurately enough of the lower classes' being "like ᶜapiru" when they assassinate or harass their lords, appropriate their land and property, form alliances with other folk in the countryside, and generally rely upon intrigue and psychological warfare rather than frontal attack.

Nor is this tactical link between social bandits and broader movements absent from the traditions of early Israel. As has been pointed out frequently (Alt 1939: 58–61; Greenberg 1955: 75–76 and n. 73; Campbell 1960: 14), the narratives about Abimelech (Judges 9), Jephthah (Judges 11), and especially David (1 Samuel 23–27; 29–30) provide excellent *social* parallels to the Amarna ᶜ*apiru* in this regard. The description of 1 Sam 22:1–2 is classic:

> David departed from there and escaped to the cave of Adullam. When his brothers and all his extended family heard it, they went down to him there. Then every man who was in straits, every man who had a pressing creditor, and every man who was embittered gathered to him, and he became their leader. About 400 men were with him.

With this band David extorted "protection money" from the rich, plundered Judah's traditional enemies, shared the spoil with the village elders, curried the favor of cities and kings as their mercenary and enfeoffed vassal, (always playing "both ends against the middle"), and thereby built the nucleus of power around which the monarchic state of Israel was formed.

Neither the Amarna corpus nor the Hebrew Bible provides as much information about such activities as one might wish because the ultimate composers of each were primarily concerned with other matters and perspectives. Even so, this brief investigation has found unequivocal evidence in the letters of both flourishing social banditry and a broader social unrest. The former served the latter as symptom, symbiotic ally, and tactical model. Although the Syrian movement apparently eventuated in little because of opportunistic leadership and cooptation and intervention by Hittite power, what Egyptian presence there was in Palestine hardly touched the hinterlands, even at moments of maximum strength. Can there have been no continuity, therefore, between the social dynamic of Amarna-Age Palestine and that of the formation of Israel, when premonarchic Israel's primary areas of strength, its enemies, and its forms of social organization were all congruent with those of the Amarna ᶜ*apiru* and their allies?

BIBLIOGRAPHY

Aharoni, Y.
  1967   *The Land of the Bible: A Historical Geography.* Trans. A. F. Rainey from Hebrew, 1962. Philadelphia: Westminster.
  1976   Nothing Early and Nothing Late: Re-writing Israel's Conquest. *Biblical Archaeologist* 39: 55–76.
AHw
  1965   Soden, W. von. *Akkadisches Handwörterbuch.* Wiesbaden: Harrassowitz.

84   CHANEY

Albright, W. F.
1932   *The Excavations of Tell Beit Mirsim*, Vol. 1. Annual of the American Schools of
        Oriental Research 12. New Haven: American Schools of Oriental Research.
1938   *The Excavations of Tell Beit Mirsim*, Vol. 2. Annual of the American Schools of
        Oriental Research 17. New Haven: American Schools of Oriental Research.
1943   *The Excavations of Tell Beit Mirsim*, Vol. 3. Annual of the American Schools of
        Oriental Research 21–22. New Haven: American Schools of Oriental Research.
1960   *The Archaeology of Palestine*. Rev. ed. Baltimore: Penguin.
1975   The Amarna Letters from Palestine. Pp. 98–119 in Vol. 2, Pt. 2 of *The
        Cambridge Ancient History*, 3rd ed., eds. I. E. S. Edwards; N. G. L. Hammond;
        and E. Sollberger. Cambridge: Cambridge University.
Alt, A.
1936   Josua. Pp. 13–29 in *Werden und Wesen des Alten Testaments*, ed. P. Volz;
        F. Stummer; and J. Hempel. Beihefte zur Zeitschrift für die Alttestamentliche
        Wissenschaft 66. Berlin: Töpelmann=Pp. 176–92 in Vol. 1 of *Kleine Schriften zur
        Geschichte des Volkes Israels*. Munich: Beck, 1953.
1939   Erwägungen über die Landnahme der Israeliten in Palästina. *Palästinajahrbuch
        des Deutschen evangelischen Instituts für Altertumswissenschaft des Heiligen
        Landes zu Jerusalem* 35: 8–63=Pp. 126–75 in Vol. 1 of *Kleine Schriften zur Ge-
        schichte des Volkes Israel*. Munich: Beck, 1953.
1955   Micha 2, 1–5, *GĒS ANADASMOS* in Juda. Pp. 13–23 in *Interpretations ad
        Vetus Testamentum pertinentes Sigmundo Mowinckel septuagenario missae*. Oslo:
        Forlaget Land og Kirke=Pp. 373–81 in Vol. 3 of *Kleine Schriften zur Geschichte
        des Volkes Israel*, ed. M. Noth. Munich: Beck, 1959.
1959   Der Anteil des Königtums an der sozialen Entwicklung in der Reichen Israel und
        Juda. Pp. 348–72 in Vol. 3 of *Kleine Schriften zur Geschichte des Volkes Israels*,
        ed. M. Noth. Munich: Beck.
1966   The Settlement of the Israelites in Palestine. Pp. 135–69 in *Essays on Old
        Testament History and Religion* Trans. R. A. Wilson from German, 1925, 1953.
        Oxford: Blackwell.
Artzi, P.
1964   "Vox Populi" in the el-Amarna Tablets. *Revue d'assyriologie et d'archéologie
        orientale* 58: 159–66.
Astour, M. C.
1964   The Amarna Age Forerunners of Biblical Anti-Royalism. Pp. 6–17 in *For Max
        Weinreich on His Seventieth Birthday*. The Hague: Moulton.
1976   Habiru. Pp. 382–85 in *The Interpreter's Dictionary of the Bible, Supplementary
        Volume*, ed. K. Crim. Nashville: Abingdon.
Bagnall, R. S.
1976   *The Administration of the Ptolemaic Possessions Outside Egypt*. Leiden: Brill.
Baly, D.
1963   *Geographical Companion to the Bible*. New York: McGraw-Hill.
Bess, S. H.
1963   Systems of Land Tenure in Ancient Israel. Ph.D. thesis, The University of
        Michigan.
Blum, J.
1961   *Lord and Peasant in Russia From the Ninth to the Nineteenth Century*. Princeton:
        Princeton University.
Bright, J.
1953   The Book of Joshua: Introduction and Exegesis. Pp. 541–673 in Vol. 2 of *The
        Interpreter's Bible*, ed. G. A. Buttrick. Nashville: Abingdon.
1972   *A History of Israel*. 2nd ed. Philadelphia: Westminster.

CAD
1958   *The Assyrian Dictionary*, Vol. 4, *E*, ed. I. J. Gelb *et al.* Chicago: Oriental Institute.
1964   *The Assyrian Dictionary*, Vol. 1, Pt. 1, *A*, ed. I. J. Gelb *et al.* Chicago: Oriental Institute.

Callaway, J.
1976   Excavating Ai (et-Tell): 1964–72. *Biblical Archaeologist* 39: 18–30.

Campbell, E. F.
1960   The Amarna Letters and the Amarna Period. *Biblical Archaeologist* 23: 2–22=Pp. 54–75 in Vol. 3 of *The Biblical Archaeologist Reader*, eds. E. F. Campbell and D. N. Freedman. Garden City: Doubleday, 1970.
1975   Moses and the Foundations of Israel. *Interpretation* 29: 141–54.
1976   Two Amarna Notes: The Shechem City-State and Amarna Administrative Terminology. Pp. 39–54 in *Magnalia Dei, The Mighty Acts of God: Essays on the Bible and Archaeology in Memory of G. Ernest Wright*, eds. F. M. Cross; W. E. Lemke; and P. D. Miller. New York: Doubleday.

Chaney, M. L.
1976   *ḤDL*-II and the "Song of Deborah": Textual, Philogical, and Sociological Studies in Judges 5, with Special Reference to the Verbal Occurrences of *ḤDL* in Biblical Hebrew. Ph.D. thesis, Harvard University.

Childs, B. S.
1963   A Study of the Formula, "Until This Day." *Journal of Biblical Literature* 82: 279–92.
1974   The Etiological Tale Re-examined. *Vetus Testamentum* 24: 387–97.

Cross, F. M.
1973   *Canaanite Myth and Hebrew Epic: Essays in the History of the Religion of Israel.* Cambridge, MA: Harvard University.

CTA
1963   *Corpus des tablettes en cunéiformes alphabétiques*, ed. A. Herdner. Mission de Ras Shamra 10. Paris: Imprimerie Nationale.

Dever, W. G.
1974   *Archaeology and Biblical Studies: Retrospects and Prospects.* Evanston.
1977   The Patriarchal Traditions. Pp. 70–120 in *Israelite and Judaean History*, eds. J. H. Hayes and J. M. Miller. Philadelphia: Westminster.

Diakonoff, I. M.
1975   The Rural Community in the Ancient Near East. *Journal of the Economic and Social History of the Orient.* 17: 121–33.

Dietrich, M.; Loretz, O.; and Sanmartín, J.
1974   Zur ugaritischen Lexikographie (XI). *Ugarit-Forschungen* 6: 19–38.

Forbes, R. J.
1972   *Studies in Ancient Terminology*, Vol. 9. 2nd ed. Leiden: Brill.

Freedman, D. N.
1976   Deuteronomic History. Pp. 226–28 in *The Interpreter's Dictionary of the Bible, Supplementary Volume*, ed. K. Crim. Nashville: Abingdon.

Frick, F. S.
1971   The Rechabites Reconsidered. *Journal of Biblical Literature* 90: 279–87.

Fritz, V.
1969   Die sogenannte Liste der besiegten Könige in Joshua 12. *Zeitschrift des Deutschen Palästina-Vereins* 85: 136–61.

Geus, C. H. J. de
1975   The Importance of Agricultural Terraces, with an Excursus on the Hebrew word *gbī*. *Palestine Exploration Quarterly* 107: 65–74.

1976   *The Tribes of Israel*. Studia semitica Neerlandica 18. Assen. Van Gorcum.
Gottwald, N. K.
1974   Were the Early Israelites Pastoral Nomads? Pp. 223–55 in *Rhetorical Criticism:
            Essays in Honor of James Muilenburg*, eds. J. J. Jackson and M. Kessler.
            Pittsburgh Theological Monograph Series 1. Pittsburgh: Pickwick Press.
1975   Domain Assumptions and Societal Models in the Study of Pre-Monarchic Israel.
            Pp. 89–100 in *Supplements to Vetus Testamentum* 18. Leiden: Brill.
1976a   Israel, Social and Economic Development of. Pp. 465–68 in *The Interpreter's
            Dictionary of the Bible, Supplementary Volume*, ed. K. Crim. Nashville:
            Abingdon.
1976b   Nomadism. Pp. 629–31 in *The Interpreter's Dictionary of the Bible, Supple-
            mentary Volume*, ed. K. Crim. Nashville: Abingdon.
1978a   The Hypothesis of the Revolutionary Origins of Ancient Israel: A Response to
            Hauser and Thompson. *Journal for the Study of the Old Testment* 7: 37–52.
1978b   Were the Early Israelites Pastoral Nomads? *Biblical Archaeological Review* 4:
            2–7.
Greenberg, M.
1955   The *Ḫab/piru*. American Oriental Series 39. New Haven: American Oriental
            Society.
1962   Crimes and Punishments. Pp. 733–44 in Vol. 1 of *The Interpreter's Dictionary of
            the Bible*, ed. G. A. Buttrick. Nashville: Abingdon.
Halpern, B.
1975   Gibeon: Israelite Diplomacy in the Conquest Era. *The Catholic Biblical Quarterly*
            37: 303–16.
Harris, M.
1968   *The Rise of Anthropological Theory: A History of Theories of Culture*. New
            York: Crowell.
Hauser, A. J.
1978a   Israel's Conquest of Palestine: A Peasants' Rebellion? *Journal for the Study of
            the Old Testament* 7: 2–19.
1978b   Response to Thompson and Mendenhall. *Journal for the Study of the Old
            Testment* 7: 35–36.
Helck, W.
1962   *Die Beziehungen Ägyptens zu Vorderasien im 3. und 2. Jahrtausend v. Chr.*
            Ägyptologische Abhandlungen 5. Wiesbaden: Harrassowitz.
Heltzer, M.
1976   *The Rural Community in Ancient Ugarit*. Wiesbaden: Reichert.
Hobsbawm, E. J.
1965   *Primitive Rebels: Studies in Archaic Forms of Social Movement in the 19th and
            20th Centuries*. New York: Norton.
1969   *Bandits*. New York: Delacorte.
1973   Social Banditry. Pp. 142–57 in *Rural Protest: Peasant Movements and Social
            Change*, ed. H. A. Landsberger. New York: Barnes & Nobel.
Holladay, W. L.
1973   The Kingdom of Yahweh. *Interpretation* 27: 269–74.
Knudtzon, J. A.
1915   *Die El-Amarna-Tafeln*. 2 vols. Leipzig: Hinrichs. Reprinted Aalen: Zeller, 1964.
Köhler, L.
1956   *Hebrew Man*. Trans. P. R. Ackroyd from German, 1953. Nashville: Abingdon.
Kupper, J. -R.
1957   *Les nomades en Mesopotamie au temps des rois de Mari*. Bibliothèque de la
            Faculté de Philosophie et Lettres de l'Université de Liege 142. Paris: Société de
            l'Édition "Les Belles Lettres."

Landsberger, B. H., and Landsberger, H. A.
1973   The English Peasant Revolt of 1381. Pp. 95–141 in *Rural Protest: Peasant Movements and Social Change*, ed. H. A. Landsberger. New York: Barnes & Noble.
Landsberger, H. A.
1969   The Role of Peasant Movements and Revolts in Development. Pp. 1–61 in *Latin American Peasant Movements*, ed. H. A. Landsberger. Ithaca: Cornell University.
1973   Peasant Unrest: Themes and Variations. Pp. 1–64 in *Rural Protest: Peasant Movements and Social Change*, ed. H. A. Landsberger. New York: Barnes & Noble.
Lapp, P. W.
1967   The Conquest of Palestine in the Light of Archaeology. *Concordia Theological Monthly* 38: 283–300.
1969a   *Biblical Arahaeology and History*. New York: World.
1969b   The 1968 Excavations at Tell Taᶜannek. *Bulletin of the American Schools of Oriental Research* 195: 2–49.
Latron, A.
1936   *La vie rurale en Syrie et au Liban: etude d'économie sociale*. Beirut: Imprimerie Catholique.
Lenski, G. E.
1966   *Power and Privilege: A Theory of Social Stratification*. New York: McGraw-Hill.
1976   History and Social Change. *American Journal of Sociology* 82: 548–64.
Lenski, G., and Lenski, J.
1978   *Human Societies: An Introduction to Macrosociology*. 3rd ed. New York: McGraw-Hill.
Liverani, M.
1965   Implicazioni sociali nella politica di Abdi-Ashirta di Amurru. *Rivista degli Studi Orientali* 40: 267–77.
1974   La Royauté syrienne de l'âge du bronze récent. *Recontre assyriologie internationale* 19: 329–56.
Long, B. O.
1968   *The Problem of Etiological Narrative in the Old Testament*. Beihefte zur Zeitschrift für die Alttestamentliche Wissenschaft 108. Berlin: Töpelmann.
Lorton, D.
1974   *The Juridical Terminology of International Relations in Egyptian Texts through Dyn. XVIII*. Baltimore: Johns Hopkins.
Luke, J. T.
1965   Pastoralism and Politics in the Mari Period: A Re-Examination of the Character and Political Significance of the Major West Semitic Tribal Groups of the Middle Euphrates. Ph.D. thesis, The University of Michigan.
McCarter, P. K.
1973   Rib-Adda's Appeal to Aziru (*EA* 162, 1–21). *Oriens Antiquus* 12: 15–18.
Maddin, R.; Muhly, J. D.; and Wheeler, T. S.
1977   How the Iron Age Began. *Scientific American* 237: 122–31.
Mendenhall, G. E.
1947   The Message of Abdi-Ashirta to the Warriors, *EA* 74. *Journal of Near Eastern Studies* 6: 123–24.
1954   Ancient Oriental and Biblical Law. *Biblical Archaeologist* 17: 26–46= Pp. 1–24 in Vol. 3 of *The Biblical Archaeologist Reader*, eds. E. F. Campbell and D. N. Freedman. Garden City: Doubleday, 1970.
1962   The Hebrew Conquest of Palestine. *Biblical Archaeologist* 25: 66–87.
1970   The Hebrew Conquest of Palestine. Pp. 100–20 in Vol. 3 of *The Biblical Archaeologist Reader*, eds. E. F. Campbell and D. N. Freedman= Slight revision of *Biblical Archaeologist* 25: 66–87.

1973   *The Tenth Generation: The Origins of the Biblical Tradition.* Baltimore: Johns Hopkins University.

1975a   The Conflict Between Value Systems and Social Control. Pp. 169–80 in *Unity and Diversity: Essays in the History, Literature, and Religion of the Ancient Near East,* eds. H. Goedicke and J. J. M. Roberts. Baltimore: Johns Hopkins University.

1975b   The Monarchy. *Interpretation* 29: 155–70.

1976a   "Change and Decay in All Around I See": Conquest, Covenant, and *The Tenth Generation. Biblical Archaeologist* 39: 152–57.

1976b   Social Organization in Early Israel. Pp. 132–51 in *Magnalia Dei. The Mighty Acts of God: Essays on the Bible and Archaeology in Memory of G. Ernest Wright,* eds. F. M. Cross, W. E. Lemke, and P. D. Miller. New York: Doubleday.

1978   Between Theology and Archaeology. *Journal for the Study of the Old Testament* 7: 28–34.

Miller, J. M.

1977   The Israelite Occupation of Canaan. Pp. 213–84 in *Israelite and Judaean History,* eds. J. H. Hayes and J. M. Miller. Philadelphia: Westminster.

Moore, B.

1966   *Social Origins of Dictatorship and Democracy: Lord and Peasant in the Making of the Modern World.* Boston: Beacon.

Moore, G. F.

1895   *A Critical and Exegetical Commentary on Judges.* The International Critical Commentary. Edinburgh: Clark.

Moran, W. L.

1953   Amarna *ŠUMMA* in Main Clauses. *Journal of Cuneiform Studies* 7: 78–80.

1967   Habiru (Habiri). pp. 878b–80b in Vol. 6 of *New Catholic Encyclopedia.* Washington: Catholic University.

1969   The Death of ʿAbdi-Aširta. *Eretz-Israel* 9: 94–99.

1975   The Syrian Scribe of the Jerusalem Amarna Letters. Pp. 146–66 in *Unity and Diversity: Essays in the History, Literature, and Religion of the Ancient Near East,* eds. II. Goedicke and J. J. M. Roberts. Baltimore: Johns Hopkins University.

Nicholson, E. W.

1973   *Exodus and Sinai in History and Tradition.* Growing Points in Theology. Richmond: John Knox.

Noth, M.

1953   *Das Buch Josua.* 2nd ed. Handbuch zum Alten Testament 7. Tübingen: Mohr.

1960   *The History of Israel.* 2nd ed. Trans. P. R. Ackroyd from German, 1958. New York: Harper & Row.

1966   The Laws in the Pentateuch: Their Assumptions and Meaning. Pp. 1–107 in *The Laws in the Pentateuch and Other Essays.* Trans. D. R. Ap-Thomas from German, 1940, 1957, 1960. Edinburgh: Oliver & Boyd.

Parsons, T.

1977   *The Evolution of Societies,* ed. and with an introduction by J. Toby. Foundations of Modern Sociology Series. Englewood Cliffs: Prentice-Hall.

Paul, S. M.

1970   *Studies in the Book of the Covenant in the Light of Cuneiform and Biblical Law.* Supplements to Vetus Tetamentum 18. Leiden: Brill.

Paul, S. M., and Dever, W. G., eds.

1973   *Biblical Archaeology.* The New York Times Library of Jewish Knowledge. New York: Quadrangle.

Pintore, F.

1972   Transiti di truppe e schemi epistolari nella Siria egiziana dell'età di el-Amarna. *Oriens Antiquus* 11: 101–31.

1973   La prassi della marcia armata nella Siria egiziana dell'età di el-Amarna. *Oriens Antiquus* 12: 299–318.

Rainey, A. F.
1970   *El Amarna Tablets 359–379: Supplement to J. A. Knudtzon, Die El-Amarna-Tafeln*. Alter Orient und Altes Testament 8. Neukirchen-Vluyn: Neukirchener Verlag.

Riemann, P. A.
1963   Desert and Return to Desert in the Pre-exilic Prophets. Ph.D. thesis, Harvard University.

Rowton, M. B.
1965   The Topological Factor in the *Ḫapiru* Problem. Pp. 375–87 in *Studies in Honor of Benno Landsberger*, eds. H. G. Güterbock and T. Jacobsen. Assyriological Studies 16. Chicago: University of Chicago.
1976a   Dimorphic Structure and the Problem of the ʿApirû-ʿIbrîm. *Journal of Near Eastern Studies* 35: 13–20.
1976b   Dimorphic Structure and Topology: *Oriens Antiquus* 15: 17–31.
1977   Dimorphic Structure and the Parasocial Element. *Journal of Near Eastern Studies* 36: 181–98.

Sasson, J. M.
1974   Review of *The Tenth Generation: The Origins of the Biblical Tradition*, by G. E. Mendenhall. *Journal of Biblical Literature* 93: 294–96.

Seeligmann, I. L.
1961   Aetiological Elements in Biblical Historiography. *Zion* 26: 141–69 (Hebrew).

Sjoberg, G.
1960   *The Preindustrial City: Past and Present*. New York: Free Press.

Soggin, J. A.
1972   *Joshua: A Commentary*. Trans. R. A. Wilson from French, 1970. Philadelphia: Westminster.

Stager, L. E.
1976   Agriculture. Pp. 11–13 in *The Interpreter's Dictionary of the Bible, Supplementary Volume*, ed. K. Crim. Nashville: Abingdon.

Talmon, S.
1966   The "Desert Motif" in the Bible and in Qumran Literature. Pp. 31–63 in *Biblical Motifs: Origins and Transformations*, ed. A. Altmann. Cambridge, MA: Harvard University.

Tcherikover, V.
1959   *Hellenistic Civilization and the Jews*. Trans. S. Applebaum from Hebrew. New York: Jewish Publication Society. Reprinted New York: Atheneum, 1970.

Thompson, T. L.
1978   Historical Notes on "Israel's Conquest of Palestine: A Peasants' Rebellion?" *Journal for the Study of the Old Testament* 7: 20–27.

Tucker, G. M.
1972   The Rahab Saga (Joshua 2): Some Form-Critical and Traditio-Historical Observations. Pp. 66–86 in *The Use of the Old Testament in the New and Other Essays: Studies in Honor of William Franklin Stinespring*, ed. J. M. Efird. Durham: Duke University.

Weber, M.
1952   *Ancient Judaism*. Trans. H. H. Gerth and D. Martindale from German, 1917–19, 1921. New York: Free Press.

Weippert, M.
1971   *The Settlement of the Israelite Tribes in Palestine*. Studies in Biblical Theology, 2nd ser., 21. Trans. J. D. Martin from German, 1967. London: SCM.
1974   Semitische Nomaden des zweiten Jahrtausends: Über die Šȝśw der ägyptischen Quellen. *Biblica* 55: 265–80, 427–33.

1976   Canaan, Conquest and Settlement of. Pp. 125–30 in *The Interpreter's Dictionary of the Bible, Supplementary Volume*, ed. K. Crim. Nashville: Abingdon.

Wiseman, D. J.
1953   *The Alalakh Tablets*. London: The British Institute of Archaeology at Ankara.

Wolf, E. R.
1966   *Peasants*. Foundations of Modern Anthropology Series. Englewood Cliffs: Prentice-Hall.
1969   *Peasant Wars of the Twentieth Century*. New York: Harper & Row.

Wright, G. E.
1962   *Biblical Archaeology*. Rev. ed. Philadelphia: Westminster.

Yadin, Y.
1963   *The Art of Warfare in Biblical Lands*. 2 vols. New York: McGraw-Hill.

Ancient Israel's Hyphenated History

George E. Mendenhall

It has been just twenty years since my brief programmatic article on the Israelite "conquest" of Palestine appeared in the *Biblical Archaeologist* (Mendenhall 1962). The stated purpose was "to suggest further fruitful lines of inquiry, and to suggest relationships between seemingly unrelated bits of information." The events that had been described as the Israelite "conquest" actually represented the "withdrawal of large population groups from any obligation to the existing political regimes," and "what happened instead may be termed, from the point of view of the secular historian interested only in socio-political processes, a peasant's revolt against the network of interlocking Canaanite city states."

I was quite aware at the time that the thesis could be subjected to exploitation by political propagandists interested only in "socio-political processes," and now we have a large work that systematically attempts to force the ancient historical data into the Procrustes' Bed of nineteenth century Marxist sociology. My attempts to warn against such reductionistic interpretations of the history of a society radically different from that of the nineteenth century after the industrial revolution, are derided by Gottwald in his magnum opus *The Tribes of Yahweh*, together with most of biblical scholarship and biblical theology as "idealistic," "mystifying," and "unscientific."

Only a couple months ago I asked one of our most eminent sociologists whether modern sociology could be used as the basis for reconstructing an ancient society. The response was a vigorous negative. The same has been observed even with reference to ancient Roman society, which is far more contiguous and continuous with our own culture, than is the biblical society of the ancient Near East (MacMullen 1974: 89). What Gottwald has actually produced is a modern version of the ancient myth-making mentality. Utilizing both the terminology and the driving ideas of a nineteenth century political ideology, he proceeds blithely to read into biblical history whatever is called for in the program of that nineteenth century ideology.

To put it bluntly, Gottwald's method is exactly that of any latter day fundamentalist. The procedure is first to place a blind faith in the absolute inerrancy of the nineteenth century ideological system, so that nothing in the Bible can possibly disagree with that system. Next, explicate the Bible to show how that system "explains" everything that needs to be explained. Finally, use the results and the authority of the Bible to clobber the opposition, and save mankind from whatever demonic malevolent social forces

91

the scholar happens to dislike. In the process, of course, anything that doesn't fit the system is either explained away, or more often quietly ignored. Gottwald's "scientific" account of the "liberated" tribes of Yahweh consists largely of an endless series of hyphenated pseudo-social science terms (on one page by actual count there were 14 hyphens and 14 periods) foisted with limitless faith upon the hapless ancient tribesmen who unfortunately were too benighted to know that they were conforming to the canons of a nineteenth century ideology. Gottwald's work should have been dedicated to George Orwell, whose picture of political bureaucrats rewriting history to make it fit a political party line is remarkably apt in 1983.

The little article on the Israelite "conquest" used the term 'peasant's revolt' only once, unless I am mistaken. In publications since then, I have emphasized in many ways that the Israelite movement was much more a cultural and ideological revolution than a political one (Mendenhall 1974: 24–26). At present that seems to be even more cogent, as information about the civilization-wide situation at the transition from the Late Bronze Age to the Early Iron Age becomes available. The cultural traits of early Israel that we can know demonstrate beyond question that it was actually a new synthesis that transformed and re-formed what already existed in Palestine in the Late Bronze Age, and therefore there cannot have been introduced a new population element that contrasted in any significant way to others of the Eastern Mediterranean region. In view of the bitter hostility to the pagan urban and political ideologies that are termed "Baal-worship," and in view of the fact that the Israelite federation had no cities worthy the name of which we have any knowledge, it seemed reasonable to assume that the polarization between Yahwists and Baal-worshipers corresponded to the contrast between urban and village culture. Gottwald has elaborated on this contrast, but unfortunately foisted upon it a nineteenth century ideology that is not only an anachronism, but worse an obscuring of what was really important about the entire social and religious movement.

Perhaps what is worst about this work is its total lack of historical perspective—and this is an inevitable consequence of his ideological system that has spelled out in advance what must be. His cultural-material ideology demands technological innovation to explain change, so he finds it in iron tools (a Philistine monopoly according to the biblical text), in terracing, and in waterproof cisterns. Since there is every reason to believe that these technological changes were constants, then all of the Near East from Greece to Yemen should have become Yahwist. Gottwald is evidently entirely innocent of any understanding of the fact that all through ancient history we know next to nothing of the daily life and society of the submerged 80% of all populations.

"Retribalization" is also an absurdity, for there is again every reason to believe that social unities that could be termed "tribes" are a constant below the political/bureaucratic level that is almost the only one we know. "Egalitarian" is also an absurdity, and there is widespread agreement among jurists at least that it is an "empty," meaningless political propaganda slogan. There is no word in biblical Hebrew that can be thus translated, and there is plenty of terminology that indicates the opposite even in the earliest sources. Ancient Israel did have the institution of slavery, and social distinctions between the affluent and the poor. That there were, other than slavery, no institutionalized rank gradations may be granted, but this is characteristic of village and tribal organization—again a constant, and probably a function in part of the generally very depressed state of the economy that was worldwide at this time. In other words, the economy everywhere was not much above the survival level.

The problem of Gottwald is that his liberated "tribes" are liberated also from virtually any substance or cultural content, once "egalitarianism" is disposed of. They evidently had a covenant, but there was no content to that either, until the Deuteronomist miraculously put himself into a time machine to resurrect faithfully the Late Bronze Age covenant structure that had been obsolete in the outside world for six centuries. They had to have a covenant renewal ceremony for which there is no direct evidence at all, and they thus constituted the "chosen people," a phrase that was not even coined until some six hundred years after the formation of the tribal Federation.

His description of the social structure is derived largely from his ideal model. Not only is there no evidence that the *bet ʾav* is an "extended family," it is questionable whether that particular type of economic organization even existed in the ancient as it does not in the modern Near East. His interpretation of *mishpaḥot* as "clans" ignores the fact that such terms both in ancient and in modern languages are not used with precision; in biblical Hebrew it can designate anything from a nuclear family to the entire Federation (cf. "family" in modern English). His system is a straitjacket that ignores what doesn't fit, because his myth demands that "it must be so." The repeated account of Zelophehad's daughters proves beyond question that the ancient Israelites were not characterized by a single, unitary social structure, and anyone with experience outside Western culture would know better than to try to impose a precision upon a very complex society that could not have been characterized by the sort of homogenized uniformity that his myth demands.

Gottwald ignores the fact that the basic social unit of early Israel is the agricultural and pastoral village. Though his own thesis demands this conclusion, he barely mentions the village unit in his discussion in spite of the fact that probably 75% of the gentilics in biblical Hebrew are village derivations. It is the village that furnishes the social context and "identity" of persons, probably the support group both socially and economically, and from the evidence of the earliest law collection, is the normal social unit involved in the administration of law.

It should be clear from any intelligent reading that Gottwald is no more interested in the concrete realities of the ancient biblical world than is any other type of fundamentalist. In fact he states flatly his program in a footnote toward the end of the book: "to start out from the present social struggle in society and church—is the correct method" (Gottwald 1979: 801 note 644). But to parade this sort of systematic anachronism as "scientific" is to make a parody of biblical studies, from which the Bible has already suffered far too much.

Gottwald's mythical divine timeless pattern demands that before the "revolution" there must have been a "feudal" society, and therefore the Canaanite city states were naturally a feudalism from which the "liberated" tribes were delivered with the aid, of course, of an enlightened Marxist ideology. What actually happened is almost totally irrelevant to this pseudo-historical propaganda. Though it is obvious that a vast range of uncertainties still exist—of which one would hardly be aware from a reading of Gottwald's "scientific" history—the main outlines of the events that far transcend the mere happenings in Palestine of the thirteenth century B.C. seem to be as reasonably clear as can be expected in present circumstances. To give a picture of what happened demands, however, a wealth of insights to which the tired old nineteenth century sociological theories can make very little, if any contribution.

First, from everything that we know, it is just as useless to term the Canaanite culture "feudal" as it is to term the Israelite Federation an "amphictyony." Though there is no direct evidence, it is extremely probable that in every Canaanite state the political entity was conceived to be the ultimate owner of all the means of production—in other words, the real estate, in the ancient predominantly agricultural and pastoral economy. In addition, the state (which is of course, the king) was the ultimate repository of all wisdom, and therefore controlled the economy. An enormous, relatively speaking, bureaucracy was the means through which the "command economy" as Heilbronner puts it was administered: the centralized political control of the production and distribution of goods. To this the thousands of economic texts from Ur via Mari to Ugarit are most eloquent witness. The social stratification that Gottwald so deplores was the direct and it seems inevitable result of a long-continued political and bureaucratic system in which family dynasties tend to become self-perpetuating in positions of power. In addition, the military organization with its necessary "chain of command" cannot but enforce powerfully the social stratification, especially when it is so intimately bound up with both the political bureaucracy and even the priesthood.

In other words, what we are describing is the classical structure of a typical bureaucratic socialism in its broad outlines, but one that had long been entrenched in power. This, however, is by no means the simple end of the story. Already in the Late Bronze Age, a very considerable number of those Syro-Palestinian socialist regimes had been taken over by newcomers from the North. The wealth of Hurrian and Indo-European names represented in the royal onomastics proves that beyond doubt. This was true in the Amarna period already, and though we have no direct extra-biblical evidence that is useful, the takeover by the arrival of armed bands from Anatolia and northern Syria at the transition from the Late Bronze to the Early Iron Age must have been much more massive. The Philistine domination simply happens to be the tip of the iceberg, for we know of similar exotic regimes at Dor in the time of Wen-Amun, and from archaeological evidence at Ras Ibn-Hani north of Ras esh-Shamra on the northern Mediterranean coast of Syria. The regimes of Sihon with his northern Syrian titulary "King of the Amorites," and of Og as well as many other of the petty "kingdoms" listed in Joshua 10 are almost certainly illustrations of similar exotic sea- and land-based pirate groups who moved into the power vacuum left by the collapse of the Empires and the radical destruction or weakening of the old city states. The process described by MacMullen (1974: 35) differed only in scale and degree of bureaucratic organization:

> . . .first, initial conquest by the Romans; next, the rapid confiscation of all hidden weapons; [Cf. Judg. 5:8!] then, the assessment by the conquerors of what they have gained so as to exploit its riches methodically; the consternation of the censused; and thereafter recurrent spasms of protest against the weight of tribute harshly calculated and still more harshly exacted.

The ideology of these newcomers was a part of the common theology of the ancient Near East: what the king conquered by superior military power became *de facto* the property of the king, and since the king was the State the result was State-Socialism established by superior military power. The peasantry who tilled the soil and produced the goods that made possible the political and military bureaucracy had no recourse—for nothing else existed as a political alternative at that time. The formation of the Federation of ancient Israel constituted precisely the creation of an alternative that was badly needed by everyone but the elite of the bureaucratic state, but that in turn was not remotely possible until the disintegration of those military dictatorships under circumstances that we cannot yet determine with any definite and persuasive detail. When the political structure disintegrates the literate intelligentsia are the first to be regarded as dispensable, so we have no written sources that describe the process.

That the initial destructions at the end of the Late Bronze Age had nothing to do with the Israelite Federation ought to be quite clear to all. The disintegration was civilization-wide, though not simultaneous in all the civilized regions of the Near East. There was probably an incredible "fruit-basket upset" all over the Eastern and probably the Western Mediterranean region as well. The parochialism, or even academic glaucoma, that makes scholars physically incapable of taking into consideration evidence outside their own narrow field of specialization is intensified by a priori political commitments that demand scholarly conformity to parochial political or religious ideologies. Consequently, the implications of the overall catastrophe that took place at the beginning of biblical history have evidently escaped the attention of biblical scholars.

Linguistic history is one powerful way of getting inside the historical process of this exceedingly traumatic period. The unquestionable close connection of biblical Hebrew with Ugaritic has been known now for over fifty years, but the differences as well as the similarities have never been subjected to close scrutiny within the framework of social and linguistic history. These two sub-disciplines are inseparable—each is an aspect of the other. The enormous changes from the 13th century Ugaritic to the 12th century Old Poetry of the Hebrew Bible, cannot be explained merely on the basis of some mythical "language of the Hebrew people"—who did not exist until the 12th century, as will be argued below.

It is not sufficiently realized, nor the implications taken into consideration, that the same process took place with regard to every other language that we know in the ancient world. There was some excuse in the nineteenth century, when virtually nothing was known of the pre-Greek world outside the Bible and Josephus, for thinking that every time a "new" language came on the scene, there was an infusion of "fresh, unspoiled barbarian blood" from the recesses of some barbarian reservoir of populations waiting for their appearance on the scene of history. It is now impossible. If the entire phonetic and grammatical structure of Canaanite changed radically in two centuries, this differs from the evidence everywhere else only in the extremely brief gap in the linguistic evidence involved in West Semitic.

Mycenean Linear B changed radically before it became Homeric Greek or other dialects. Hurrian was so transformed, as was also Hittite, that only very recently has it been recognized that there is some continuity into later Urartean and Lydian. Luwian, like South Canaanite, does not exhibit such a time gap in attestation, but even so only quite recently has it been generally conceded that it has a continuity in the Lycian inscriptions of southern Anatolia beginning about the fifth century.

The changes were so enormous in every case that some diehard scholars are still challenging the continuities now generally accepted. Underlying those changes was, however, a social history that has not really become the subject for investigation. There has been no method for doing so—and there cannot be until the scholarly world realizes that cultural history and political history are two quite distinct and equally important fields of investigation. The linguistic changes described above seem totally inexplicable and mysterious only because philologians dealing with ancient languages have almost entirely separated language study from human beings and human culture. The linguistic changes in South Canaanite seem so great only because the LB written sources stem from an educated bureaucratic elite, while the language of the earliest sources of Hebrew Bible stem from non-elite, village dialect regions. Between these two elements of any stratified complex civilization there is an enormous linguistic gap, and often enough, as with the Latin of the Middle Ages, there was a total linguistic hiatus. Fortunately, we have evidence from the late Ugaritic prose texts, that the elegant language of the mythical and epic texts was not that of the man in the street, and it seems that at least one bureaucrat of the Ugaritic regime tried to spell words the way people actually were speaking in the thirteenth century Ugarit.

The linguistic gap is thus partly due to the disappearance of the educated elite with the destruction of the stratified political systems of the Late Bronze Age. Enormously hastening the linguistic change was the immigration from the North of an already very composite population fleeing the catastrophes that virtually depopulated central Anatolia and at least parts of inland northern Syria. There arose a *lingua franca* all over the eastern Mediterranean region, and only in the inland southern fringe areas, so far as our evidence now goes, was there a continuity of the Bronze Age linguistic structure, which in the Iron Age is identified as the various regional dialects of pre-Islamic Arabic. It follows that the population of Palestine prior to the Early Iron Age, and the rapid transformation of West Semitic spoke a language that in all essential features may be identifiable as proto-Arabic. Furthermore, the early stages of the transformation were already in process in urban environments at least by the thirteenth century. The rapidity of the change is best accounted for by the hypothesis of migration from the non-Semitic speaking northern (Anatolian) populations, of which the Philistines are merely the best attested. The fact that biblical Hebrew contains only about 5% of vocabulary items that have no cognates in other Semitic languages is proof of the fact that there cannot have been any significant change in population that was not also a constant in the Eastern Mediterranean world. This process of linguistic change of so great a magnitude that it results in a new linguistic system may be termed "creolization," an excellent example of which has been thoroughly described for Nicaragua's Miskito Coast (Holm 1982).

At the same time, there is no conceivable situation that would justify any idea that the Twelve Tribe Federation was characterized by any linguistic homogeneity, and the extremely valuable *shibboleth* narrative proves what must be expected. It is for this reason that unilinear evolutionary patterns in linguistic usage in the Old Poetry of the Bible are monuments to modern scholarly ingenuity, but not historically grounded reliable conclusions. It is not until there is a prestigious cadre of the educated that an official "correctness" of spelling, grammar, and orthography can be created —that is, with the monarchy, under which the production of written documents probably also occurred for the first time.

Even then, ironically enough, the standard language of South Canaanite that we are wont to term "biblical Hebrew" was, as all have admitted, the language of urban Jerusalem, which was not even a specifically "Israelite" dialect. It is for this reason that we have difficulties in treating texts that clearly do not stem from, nor were rewritten in that standard language of the political establishment. The fact that we have not been able to see any considerable dialect difference is tribute to the fact that there were very minor "ethnic" linguistic contrasts between the urban and rural, i.e., polytheist and Yahwist populations, by the end of the eleventh century: all spoke a variety of local realizations of the *lingua franca* that is attested as far away as Sardinia.

The arguments presented in the foregoing paragraphs should make it clear that Gottwald's class-struggle elaboration is almost totally irrelevant to the historical processes involved in the events that ranged from about 1250 to 1100 B.C. The linguistic evidence alone makes it virtually impossible to place any of the biblical materials and traditions securely into the thirteenth century B.C. or earlier except for the radically re-adapted "patriarchal" narratives and a few other reminiscences of ancient pre-Yahwist traditions. The picture we have of the context of earliest Israel, politically speaking, is one almost totally other than that of Amarna Canaan, which is the best attested earlier condition that we know. The narratives dealing with the South and with Transjordan depict a situation that fits by far best into the initial stages of the Iron Age, ca. 1200 to 1150 B.C., and with that context for the formation of the Israelite Federation it would seem that very many historical, social, and archaeological data fall fairly neatly into place.

The historical situation at the formation of the Twelve Tribe Federation may be posited somewhat as follows: (It is necessary to point out that this is no "idealism" like that of Gottwald's "ideal model." It is curious that his "models" are never "ideal." They are always "scientific.")

1. The destruction levels of the LB city states are a generation or two in the past. The surviving cities are mere shadows of their once powerful and prosperous status. It is this fact that made possible the "military victories" of the Israelite peasantry.

2. From the collapse of the northern cultures and empires signalled by increasing stress, many people had fled to thinly populated regions, or left the sinking ship for less stressful if more economically insecure regions: 1250–1175 B.C. The seafarers lost their home (i.e., wintertime) bases through the destruction of the northern empires and states, and had to seek new ones.

3. The thinly populated regions show considerable and sudden growth in occupation: Transjordan, Negev, Galilee.

4. The cities continue, by and large, an enormously reduced economic existence. Much of the population had to leave the city to go back to the farm. Cross-cultural trade virtually ceased.

5. All larger social organizations have collapsed; security is at a minimum. Into the power vacuum move numerous professional military bands, by sea and by land, to take over control in what is left of the "cities," and at the same time pretend to be their saviors.

6. The village population have somewhat less than enthusiasm about the prospect of being again subject to the unlimited demands of urban political military elites, and the prospect of very wide scale support from the territory-wide unity under a God whose demands are what all need is sufficient to

unify virtually all the non-urban population in a covenant of peace.

7. It worked well enough for a century and a half. By that time the intense solidarity of the Yahwist federation was waning in favor of the long traditional local autonomy and self-sufficiency, often enough accompanied by the revival of the local cults: the "Baals." The growth of the Philistine power had proceeded far enough to make the formation of a political state inevitable. There was no other way to furnish an upward mobility for those who were tired of village life, above all the hard work and low standard of living it entailed.

8. King David by military force absorbed the urban centers, thus doing away with the centuries long polarization and hostility between urban and village ideologies. He was miraculously successful for a time since the village population could identify themselves with him, and thus they furnished a much larger population base for a power structure than could possibly have been obtained by any of the old city-state power centers.

9. With Solomon the old urban centers, especially Jerusalem, became again dominant. The elaborate cultus represented a sophisticated and deliberate blend of Yahwist and age-old Syro-Palestinian ritual and theology. The bureaucracy became a mirror image of that which the Yahwist populations had rebelled against in the first place. They rebelled again—but like the sorcerer's apprentice, all they could do was cut the monster in two—they couldn't bring it to an end.

To translate this working hypothesis that should be regarded as within the framework of social and especially cultural history, rather than "sociological" as Weippert (1972) has grossly misconstrued it, into the more familiar archaeological categories I would suggest the following as a context in which the archaeological evidence fits quite well:

The destruction levels of the LB cities in Palestine are a local expression of a process that continued for a century of time and extended in space from Mycenae to Egypt, and somewhat later and it would seem with less severity in Mesopotamia. In North Syria and also in Anatolia there was a drastic reduction of population density. The deurbanization and political devolution is a constant over the entire civilized region of which we have any knowledge. As Chester Starr (1982) has recently observed with regard to the Roman Empire, "The question is not why it fell; the question is why it survived as long as it did." Perhaps the best answer to the question of the fall is simply that the economic, social, political, and military problems became so great that the system simply collapsed into violent destruction or abandonment of its own weight. It is highly probable that widespread epidemic disease also had much to do with the process.

The Iron Ia period in Palestine and Transjordan is witness to the growth of population in those regions, largely through immigration of armed bands and farm families from the North, attested in Egyptian sources. The recovery of some cities in that period is pathetic in comparison to their wealth in the LB II period, but they were pathetically trying to perpetuate the glories of their past. A large number of new settlements were established, including some walled cities in the southern Transjordan and the northwestern Hejaz (Parr 1970; Sauer 1982). These latter are almost certainly to be identified as the "Midianite" civilization, which had none but possibly historical ties to the later camel-riding Bedouin. Here also Gottwald is wrong in identifying them with the first true Bedouin, as he is also in his assertion that my objection to the "Bedouin mirage" is dependent upon the dissertation of Tracy Luke. Already when I was in graduate work at Johns Hopkins, Albright was observing the inappropriateness of theories of Bedouin origins. My own perceptions were enormously enhanced by lengthy conversations with Lawrence Krader in the summer of 1951.

The Midianite "raiders" of the Gideon story represent the same sort of camel-cavalry attested three centuries later at the Battle of Qarqar, and are merely the usual harvest season tax-collectors. They represent a very ephemeral Midianite political expansion into Palestine proper. This is most unlikely before 1200 B.C. or after 1125 B.C., when with the laconic notice in Gen 36:35 all references to Midian as an existing political entity cease.

Similar cultural traits of Iron Ia occur in both southern Palestine and southern Transjordan (Sauer 1982), and it is another example of historical naivete, or the Gottwaldian reading of a modern political myth into the archaeological evidence to identify this assemblage of pottery plus house structure with the "conquering Israelites." A now considerable number of sites reasonably well identified with those narrated in the early biblical traditions have been found to have no occupation prior to Iron Ia, and therefore the political entities that came into conflict in the earliest period of Israel should be dated decades before the Israelite Federation itself existed. The full extension of this Federation can hardly be dated earlier than 1150 B.C., therefore, and its formation did not entail any significant cultural or material innovation except with regard to the guiding ideology and the wide extent of the social solidarity.

About a generation later (i.e., ca. 1175–1150 B.C.), the constant warfare among these new military dictatorships, (cf. Num 21:27–30) and their rapacious confiscation of the products of the village peasantry, created a situation that was ripe for the introduction of a new religious drive and set of norms that was attractive to all but the ambitious sea- and land-based pirates. About the same time the most successful—or at least the best attested—of these new regimes, the Philistines, began making their characteristic ceramic wares, exactly as their counterparts were at Teima and Qurayya in the Southeast, and at Ras Ibn Hani in the far North coastal plain. We are now in Iron Ib, and about this time the process began by which most of the rural and village population rejected the old political ideologies in favor of the covenant community of Yahweh—and the result was the "people whom Yahweh created."

It goes without saying that earlier attempts at unification had been going on constantly since Abdu-Ashirta's limited and temporary success in the Amarna period. The inscription of Seti I at Karnak tells us that "The foe belonging to the Shasu are plotting rebellion. Their tribal chiefs are gathered in one place, waiting on the mountain ranges of Kharu. They have taken to clamoring and quarreling, one of them killing his fellow. They have no regard for the laws of the palace" (Wilson 1955).

These socially horizontal covenants are a constant in early (typologically) societies, and Weber's emphasis upon this is one of the few remaining observations of his sociology that remains useful in studying the pre-Greek world of the ancient Near East. It should be perfectly clear, however, that from Abdu-Ashirta on, the call to unification was usually political propaganda motivated by political ambition; all such propaganda lines promised merely the exchange of one tyranny for another of the same type—and perhaps even worse.

Why the Yahwist covenant succeeded not only in bonding an astonishingly widespread and diverse population at least for a century and a half, but also in furnishing the ideological foundations for all of Western and Near Eastern civilizations for the next three thousand years is a question that the dirt archaeologist cannot even ask—but neither can the modern social scientist. I would diffidently suggest that one reason may well have been that the primary purpose precisely was *not* bonding—it was apolitical, transpolitical if you will—to create a community characterized by the renunciation of ambition for domination. It was also characterized by scrupulous concern for reciprocity and equity, which Gottwald has mistaken for "egalitarianism." It was a society in which the potential for peace existed because by definition all members were bound to the same obligations, including that to refrain from permitting their behavior to be conditioned and driven by the envy of others' possessions.

It is difficult to sum up in a brief paragraph not only what is lacking in Gottwald's work, but also its deleterious effects in the modern scene. Perhaps the primary problem is his concept of the function of religion, as well as his concept of what religion is. One need not go very far back into history to learn that theologians long ago recognized fully that "your god is that which you fear most to lose." Gottwald's imprisonment in nineteenth century ideology prevents him from seeing that his own ideology is religion, just as much dedicated to promoting a social structure as that which he is allegedly combating.

Religion, however, is a correlative not only of social structures, but also of historical events and contexts. In fact, I would argue that historical events and situations have probably always been much more a determinant of religious attitudes than are social structures. To quote Service again, "Social structure, as a matter of fact, would seem to be the result of the workings of other factors and the cause of nothing" (Service 1962: 180).

Ancient Israelite religion came about in a context almost diametrically opposite to that which Gottwald assumes, and which his driving ideology requires. As argued here, the context of early Israel is poles apart from that of the Amarna period, for which we do have reasonably accurate documentation—but that was two hundred years in the past by the time ancient Israel had its barest beginnings as a distinct religious community and social organism—I would hesitate to say "social organization."

Gottwald's entire work with few exceptions would apply quite admirably to the ideology of the Assyrian Empire, and I argue myself that Yahweh became a symbol quite similar during the Monarchy, for the identification of god with the state if not the head of state is a constant in all ancient and modern pagan societies—what the king and his bureaucrats fear most to lose.

The ancient Israelite movement, almost certainly in common with village populations through time and space, needed protection from the king and his bureaucrats as much as they did from the enemy. The village had "no real power to protect itself at all, save against another village or a passing traveler" (MacMullen 1974: 27). It is not the idea that the god is merely the projection of the society that needs explaining, it is the opposite: but this Gottwald denies in principle because his ideology won't permit anything else.

Nevertheless, it still comes as a shock to read that "Since the primary manifestation of Yahweh is Israel itself, any misconstruction of Israel entails a misconstruction of Yahweh" (Gottwald 1979: 688). To reject this propaganda does not require any particular idealism, but simply the recognition that what the Bible calls idolatry is not mere ritual deviation, but dedication to vicious ideologies. The source of this idea is not the Bible but certain ideologues of the 1930's who no doubt were also using "scientific" 19th century sociology. The best known, though Gottwald is probably too young to remember, was Alfred Rosenberg whose position was that of official ideologist for the Nazi party. From him came the statement that "If the German Race did not exist, God would not exist."

Gottwald's attempt to present us with a historical account of the beginnings of biblical history is truly a tragic comedy of errors. He has not really succeeded in projecting himself back in time beyond the late 1930's. This world certainly needs no more of that sort of enthusiasm, for we already have far too much materialist and technological elaboration driven by ideologies that are for that very reason far worse than those of primitive tribes.

We deprecate with vague inanities
Man's inhumanity to the humanities.

BIBLIOGRAPHY

Gottwald, N. K.
1979   *The Tribes of Yahweh: A Sociology of the Religion of Liberated Israel, 1250–1050 B.C.E.* Maryknoll, N.Y.: Orbis Books.

Holm, J. A.
1982   *The Creole English of Nicaragua's Miskito Coast: Its Sociolinguistic History and a Comparative Study of Its Lexicon and Syntax.* Ann Arbor: University Microfilms.

MacMullen, R.
1974   *Roman Social Relations: 50 B.C. to A.D. 284.* New Haven and London: Yale University.

Mendenhall, G. E.
1962   The Hebrew Conquest of Palestine. *Biblical Archaeologist* 25: 66–87.
1973   *The Tenth Generation: The Origins of the Biblical Tradition.* Baltimore: The Johns Hopkins University.

Parr, P., et al.
1970   Preliminary Survey in N.W. Arabia, 1968. *London Institute of Archaeology, Bulletin* 8 & 9: 192–242

Sauer, J. A.
1982   Syro-Palestinian Archaeology, History, and Biblical Studies. *Biblical Archeologist* 45: 201–209.

Service, E. R.
1962   *Primitive Social Organization.* New York.

Starr, C. G.
·1982   *The Roman Empire, 27 B.C.–476 A.D. A Study in Survival.* Oxford and New York: Oxford University.

Weippert, M.
1967   *Die Landnahme der israelitischen Stamme.* Göttingen.

Wilson, J. A.
1955   Campaigns of Seti I in Asia. P. 254 in *Ancient Near Eastern Texts Relating to the Old Testament.* 2nd. rev. ed., ed. by J. B. Pritchard. Princeton University.

AUTHOR INDEX

Adams, R. M.   28
Aharoni, Y.   44n., 50n.
Albright, W. F.   26, 44n., 50, 59, 63, 100
Alt, A.   23, 41–42, 44, 64, 72, 83
Artzi, P.   55n., 73n.
Astour, M. C.   53n., 55n.
Bagnall, R. S.   63
Baly, D.   41
Bess, S. H.   64
Blum, J.   64n.
Bright, J.   44n., 47n., 65
Callaway, J.   60
Campbell, E. F.   21, 50n., 53, 58, 59n.,
   66n., 80, 83
Carter, H.   1
Childs, B. S.   44
Cross, F. M.   47, 69
Dever, W. G.   42, 44n.
Diakonoff, I. M.   64
Dietrich, M., Loretz, O., and Sanmartin,
   J.   74n.
Driver, G. R., and Miles, J. C.   20
Dus, J.   23
Forbes, R. J.   50
Freedman, D. N.   47
Frick, F. S.   43
Fritz, V.   69
Geus, C. H. J. de   29, 41–42, 45n., 47n.,
   50, 53, 54, 61
Glock, A.   22
Goetze, A.   12
Gottwald, N. K.   vii, 25, passim.
Greenberg, M.   21, 71, 78–81, 83
Halpern, B.   69
Harris, M.   28, 46n.
Hauser, A. J.   72n.
Helck, W.   63
Heltzer, M.   26, 33, 64
Hobsbawm, E. J.   77–82
Holladay, W. L.   51n.
Holm, J. A.   97
Jacobsen, T.   29

Jankowska, N. B.   34
Klengel, H.   26
Knudtzon, J. A.   54, 75n.
Köhler, L.   71
Kosambi, D.   26
Kupper, J. -R.   42
Landsberger, H. A.   52, 55, 59n., 61–
   67, 74n., 82
Lapp, P. W.   44–47, 50, 57–61, 67
Latron, A.   64n.
Lenski, G. E.   41, 46n., 58, 61, 65, 67
Lenski, G., and Lenski, J.   40, 46n., 51,
   58, 68n., 78n.
Liverani, M.   55n.
Long, B. O.   44
Lorton, D.   63
Luke, J. T.   42, 100
MacMullen, R.   91, 95, 102
Maddin, R., Muhly, J. D., and Wheeler,
   T. S.   50
Malamat, A.   vii
Marx, K.   26
McKenzie, J. L.   20
Meek, T. J.   8
Mendelsohn, I.   26
Mendenhall, G. E.   vii; 22, passim.
Miller, J. M.   47, 50n., 58, 61, 67
Moore, B.   62–65
Moore, G. F.   70
Moran, W. L.   55n., 73n., 74n.
Nicholson, E. W.   66n.
Noth, M.   41–42, 44, 45n., 47n., 67, 71
Parr, P. et al.   100
Parsons, T.   63
Paul, S. M.   71
Paul, S. M., and Dever, W. G.   50
Pintore, F.   80
Rainey, A.   16, 19, 54n., 75n.
Reviv, H.   33
Riemann, P. A.   43
Rodinson, M.   26
Rowley, H. H.   8

105

SUBJECT INDEX